Making it till Friday

FOURTH EDITION

Making it till Friday

FOURTH EDITION

A Guide to Successful Classroom Management

James D. Long
Appalachian State University

Virginia H. Frye
University of Tennessee

With Elizabeth W. Long
Appalachian State University—
Public School Partnership Program

Princeton Book Company, Publishers
Princeton, New Jersey

The authors gratefully acknowledge Ford Button for the cartoons that appear in this edition.

Princeton Book Company, Publishers
POB 57
Pennington, NJ 08534

Design by Design and Illustration
Typesetting by Dimensional Graphics

Library of Congress Cataloging-in-Publication Data

Long, James D., 1942–
Making it till Friday : a guide to successful classroom management / James D. Long and Virginia H. Frye with Elizabeth W. Long—4th ed.
p. cm.
Includes bibliographies and index.
ISBN 0-916622-91-6
1. Classroom management. I. Frye, Virginia H. II. Long, Elizabeth W. III. Title.
LB3013.L66 1989
371.1′024—dc20 89-10450
CIP

Contents

Preface

The current edition of *Making it till Friday* examines ideas that have proven useful to teachers over many years and also presents new trends in classroom management research. Each chapter contains material from earlier editions and something new. For example, we have retained many of the concepts that relate to strengthening desired student behavior while adding strategies for developing hardiness, maintaining optimism, enhancing happiness, developing important priorities, offering feedback, and fostering creativity. New federal legislation for the handicapped and metacognitive techniques for helping youngsters evaluate their own approaches to learning are also presented. This new edition also emphasizes the relationship between knowledge about classroom management and freedom from excessive stress.

We would like to thank Wandalyn Enix, professor of education at Montclair State College, and Nancy R. Von Boeckmann, supervisor at the Department of Education at California State University, Fullerton, for their suggestions for improving this edition. We would also like to thank Roxanne Barrett for her editorial recommendations.

Although no brief text can include every strategy known to be useful to teachers, we have tried to offer enough variety to enable teachers to begin identifying the kinds of things that might work for them and their students. But because the text is selective rather than inclusive, it should be viewed as a beginning point in your efforts to learn more about classroom management. Finally, the ideas that are offered are based on research conducted in actual classroom settings, so the book stresses practice rather than theory as such. We wish you every success in using *Making it till Friday* and hope it can help you have a successful educational career.

CHAPTER 1

Making Your Own Luck: An Introduction to Classroom Management

"Louise, you look stressed. Is something wrong?"

"Actually, I am stressed. But I didn't mean to let it show."

"Oh, we all have bad days. What's the problem?"

"It's really a combination of little things. I have one student who likes to talk back and another one who seldom completes his assignments. And I had a problem with a parent which is something I'd never expected. This just hasn't been one of my lucky days."

"Maybe your luck will change."

"Maybe."

This discussion, which may appear insignificant, identifies a number of critically important issues for teachers. First, Louise, our troubled teacher, has confirmed the presence of stress in her life. Second, she has noted the existence of minor disciplinary problems in her classroom. Third, Louise has experienced a problem that was never expected. And finally, she has wondered whether her plight might simply be a matter of luck. For many teachers, these issues can signal the beginning of even greater difficulties and will be dealt with in our introductory discussion of the dynamics of effective classroom management.

Stress and Discipline

Stress associated with discipline is a major problem for teachers. Further, stress-producing problems occur in both the early and subsequent days of teaching. Researchers Abernathy, Manera, and Wright (1985) have found that student teachers rank classroom discipline as the greatest stress-producing factor in teaching. Abernathy and her colleagues also found that teachers perceived classroom discipline to be their greatest stressor.

We do not wish to overstate the connection between stress and discipline problems. Researchers have found that disciplinary problems are not always the chief stressor for teachers. In one study (Raschke, Dedrick, Strathe, & Hawkes, 1985) among 230 elementary teachers, the teachers ranked "lack of time" as the main source of stress. Disruptive students followed as a close second. Nonteaching duties and student apathy rounded out the top four. However, if one considers disciplinary problems to include student apathy as well as disruptiveness, classroom discipline would surely top almost all teachers' list of perceived stressors. In our view, classroom problems include anything that impedes the learning process.

While potentially stressful events abound in teaching, the problems are not insurmountable. In a survey of 3,300 K–12 teachers, Feitler and Tokar (1982) found that 58 percent of the teachers listed misbehavior by *individual* pupils as the leading cause of job stress. In other words, one or two students who chronically misbehaved were generally the source of stress rather than an entire class. Still, having a few problem students per class necessitates the use of effective management strategies; otherwise, the consequences could be devastating.

Approach Problems with Confidence

Much of a teacher's success in dealing with stress and disciplinary matters relies upon confronting problems with self-confidence. Some teachers become overly anxious and fail to develop effective ways of handling problems; others approach their problems with optimism and are more successful. Why these variations exist is not always easily understood. Suzanne Kobasa (1979) provides data that appears to have relevance for teachers. She analyzed the personality structure of business executives whose scores on a stress scale predicted they would become ill due to excessive stress in their lives. Seventy-five of the executives with high stress scores subsequently reported becoming ill following stressful events. Another group of 86 with high stress scores, however, remained healthy. Kobasa noted that the hardy executives had greater *control* over

"Now about our school's number-one problem: discipline . . ."

their lives, were *committed* to their own development, and were more desirous of *challenge* than the others. In brief, the hardy executives did not view themselves as victims of circumstances. They actively approached new circumstances and used their inner resources to make the most of the challenges that they met.

At least one researcher (McEnany, 1986) has extended Kobasa's (1979) findings beyond the business world. Building on Kobasa's research, McEnany interviewed 34 teachers, each with 25 or more years of service, who had been identified as having maintained dynamic teaching careers. Among other things, McEnany found that the hardy teachers recognized the importance of others' support, were actively involved in personal and professional pursuits, felt a responsibility for creating good days at school, and desired to see their students succeed. In sum, the attitudes of the hardy teachers were very similar to the attitudes of the hardy executives: both groups valued themselves and their work.

I Wish

Carlos spent a great deal of time wishing his situation were different. He felt that his life would improve substantially if he could only remove two misbehaving students from his class. However, in lamenting his plight to a colleague, Carlos gained a new perspective. Carlos' colleague asked him how he thought he could ever improve if he were never faced with a challenge. The colleague also reminded Carlos that fewer teachers would be needed if just anyone could handle discipline problems. The colleagues humorously commented, "Thank goodness for problems. They give us a reason for being here." Carlos began to sense that wishing his problems away would not make him a better teacher.

Develop Coping Skills

The research on hardiness shows that the ability to cope with stressful conditions could be related to attitudes. But in the classroom and the business world, coping mechanisms may also be tied to management skills. Two researchers (Sharp & Forman, 1985) have used classroom management training as a means of reducing teacher anxiety. Among other strategies, classroom management training emphasized identifying problems, behavioral reinforcement, contracts, and a reduction in punitive techniques. The classroom management program was compared to a stress-inoculation program that involved muscular-relaxation training and several other strategies aimed at reducing irrational reactions to stress. Both the classroom management training and the stress-inoculation training were effective in reducing self-reported anxiety and the physical indicators of anxiety. Both also helped teachers make better use of approval and disapproval. Thus, it appears that understanding how to manage a class can alleviate problems with stress and help teachers deal with discipline issues that arise.

Misconceptions about Teaching

A review of the literature on teacher burnout (Gold, 1985), suggests that people who enter the teaching profession with uninformed or unrealistic expectations of what the job entails will experience a great deal of stress and disappointment. One might also speculate that the greater the disparity between what is expected and what is found, the greater the stress and disappointment. Part of the frustration that Louise expressed in the opening paragraphs of this chapter were a result of her misconceptions about teaching. Teaching, of course, is not the only profession that offers surprises. But both in teaching and in other professions, misconceptions can pose problems.

In a popular book devoted to helping people live more effectively, Arnold Lazarus and Allen Fay (1975) described a number of mistaken beliefs that were sources of unhappiness in people's lives. Included in their list were the notions that: (a) you should strive to be good at everything; (b) work at pleasing everybody; (c) not take chances: and (d) try to become totally independent of others. Their approach for helping people avoid and change mistaken beliefs consisted of instructions on how to rethink the beliefs and how to engage in corrective behaviors.

Teachers also hold misconceptions that can reduce their enjoyment of teaching, but avoiding those misconceptions is not always easy. Ill-founded beliefs usually begin with a semblance of truth. Unfortunately, when truth is viewed too rigidly, a fallacy can result. But the likelihood of subscribing to fallacies (or myths) can be minimized through a careful analysis of ideas that could include assessing whether an idea: (a) is an overgeneralization of known facts; (b) excludes other possibilities that might also be true; and (c) could result in unnecessary problems if followed. Finally, we acknowledge that no one holds a monopoly on truth. Ultimately, you are the one who must distinguish between fact and fiction. Listed below are a few ideas that we perceive to be misconceptions about teaching along with suggestions for avoiding them.

Myth #1: Good Teachers Don't Have Problems

The notion that good teachers don't have problems is widespread. It is perpetuated by suggestions that effective teachers can prevent all disciplinary problems by keeping students interested in learning through the use of exciting materials and classroom activities. Appealing to student interests is important and can prevent many problems, but the potential for problems extends beyond academics. Students experience difficulties at home that spill over into the classroom; students experience problems with peers during class breaks and in the classroom; and students experience mood changes that can generate problems, to name just a few. Also, on any given day, numerous interactions that could pose trouble occur between teachers and students. For example, data from a study aimed at improving classroom communications (Webster & Johnson, 1987) revealed that regular classroom teachers interacted verbally with students on an average of every 2.3 minutes trying to get one or more students to comply with their requests. It is doubtful that anyone who interacts so frequently with others can avoid problems entirely. Indeed, novice and experienced teachers alike have their share of problems.

If you are among those who believe that good teachers don't have problems, classroom management difficulties might lead you to the conclusion, "I am having a problem, I must not be a good teacher." Recognizing that every teacher has had or will have problems in managing students can help prevent disillusionment with teaching. Excellence in teaching often results from experiencing and overcoming difficult situations. All problems are not necessarily bad. Some problems can serve as impetus for change.

Putting Up a Front?

Jerry was having his share of discipline problems. And to make matters seem worse, every time he asked Maria how things were going, he got a story about how wonderful things were in Maria's classes. Jerry knew that a "How are you?" is not an invitation to complain, but Maria never seemed to acknowledge having any *problems. In fact, her consistent response was always "Just great." Although Jerry realized that what is said does not always reflect reality, he could not help wondering why some people seem afraid to admit that things sometimes go wrong for them, too.*

Myth #2: Knowledge of Subject Matter Makes a Good Teacher

Competence in one's subject area is sometimes considered to be all that is necessary for effective teaching. Unfortunately, knowledge in a specific subject area in no way insures effective sharing of that knowledge. It also does not guarantee the humane treatment of others. Studies of teacher attitudes toward behavior problems suggest that elementary teachers, who generally have more training in pedagogy and classroom management, tend to be more humanistic and less custodial in their approaches with students than high-school teachers, who are more subject-matter oriented (Cheser, McDaniel, & Cheser, 1982). Nonetheless, teachers at all grade levels can improve their disciplinary styles. For example, Cheser et al. demonstrated that a group of teachers representing all grade levels significantly improved their scores on measures of effective disciplinary styles as a result of participating in a course on classroom management.

Those who believe that competence in subject areas alone will make them effective teachers might balance their views by reflecting on the teachers who were the most effective in helping them learn. Did these teachers take a purely intellectual approach, or did they combine knowledge with supportive, reinforcement techniques? Most likely, it was the latter. We think that classroom management should rest on the philosophy that positive, caring interaction with students is just as important as the academic subjects that are being studied.

Myth #3: All Students Should Be Treated the Same

Parents occasionally complain, "My child was singled out for punishment that no one else received." This type of complaint can lead to the generalization that in order to avoid trouble all students should be treated in the same manner. Admittedly, infractions of certain school policies may result in the need for standardized punishment. However, the need to show impartiality in carrying out school policies should not take precedence in all circumstances. For example, suppose most students own home computers, while a few do not. Those who do not own computers will need more training and extra attention than those who do. Obviously, these students cannot be treated "equally." The desire for equality is really more a desire for justice than it is for sameness. And justice requires that everyone be treated adequately and fairly.

Those who fear that treating students differently might be interpreted as unfair should ask themselves whether it is fair to give students with clear-cut disadvantages no more assistance than those who come to school with decidedly unequal advantages. Moreover, students have different preferences and do not feel slighted when their needs are being met in different ways. It is only when the needs of a few are being met that students sense injustice. Try providing students choices on certain assignments or offer different rewards. You will find that students will be pleased to have the choice. Further, you might want to maintain a log recording who actually receives attention and the nature of that attention.

You may find that the students who are least in need of help are actually the ones who receive the most attention.

Who Really Gets Helped?

Are students who are slow, unattractive, and socially disadvantaged afforded fewer learning opportunities than their classroom counterparts? Clare Burstall's (1978) review of research on the influence of teacher behavior on their pupils indicates that this is the case. Burstall's research shows that good readers are called on to read more often then poor readers, that those who are more capable academically are given more opportunity to be the teachers' helper and to be in charge of classroom and playground activities than less capable students, that high achievers get more opportunities to comment in class discussions than low achievers, and that the misbehavior of attractive students is more likely to get overlooked than the same behavior by unattractive students. Students who need to be given opportunities to read, to lead, to interact, and to receive rewards for desirable behaviors seem to be the ones least likely to receive them.

Myth #4: I Can Handle All the Problems Myself

Some teachers have difficulty accepting their limits. They regard receiving help from others as a personal failure. While teachers do have a major responsibility for what occurs in their classes, no teacher can be the sole problem-solving agent in a classroom. We are not suggesting that teachers relegate their work to others, but rather that they look for opportunities to work with others who can legitimately be involved in classroom decision making. For example, one important resource for improving classroom behavior is the students themselves. In a study of fifth graders (Besalel-Azrin, Azrin, & Armstrong, 1977) student-reported problems decreased by 70 percent after only one month of getting students involved in classroom management and by 96 percent after six months. A matched group of control students showed minimal improvements until they, too, were introduced to strategies that maximized their involvement. Among other responsibilities, the students in this study assumed a large role in developing a contract for social and academic behavior, in determining rewards for appropriate classroom behavior, and in correcting their mistakes and misbehavior by practicing the correct mode of behavior.

Teachers should develop a list of resource people in the school and community. You would want to include the school psychologist, counselor, nurse, and other special personnel on your list because they can assist in alleviating many behavior problems. Certainly parents who could assist in volunteer work should also be identified. Strategies for working cooperatively with parents and other professionals will be discussed in more detail in Chapter 6. At this point, you need only to identify people to assist you in your efforts with students.

A Helping Hand

By the time he reached seventh grade, Joe was seriously behind his peers in reading. As a result, he was experiencing difficulty in all academic areas and was falling further and further below grade level. Ms. Tessler, his teacher, decided that Joe would be more appropriately placed in a special education class than in a regular seventh-grade class where he could not keep up with other students. It was evident that his efforts were resulting in much frustration, and she felt that he was beginning to have emotional problems.

A referral to Mr. Blackwell, the school psychologist, was initiated, and he arranged to see and evaluate Joe. The results of the evaluation indicated that Joe's intellectual ability was normal. Mr. Blackwell arranged for more extensive evaluation to determine the cause of Joe's learning disability and to assist in planning remedial learning activities. Joe was not appropriate for placement in a special education class; however, assistance from a learning resource teacher was arranged.

Myth #5: There's Nothing I Can Do

The pessimistic antithesis of Myth #4 is the notion that there is little or nothing one can do to change students who have been negatively influenced by their home, community, or peer group. A student's environment certainly contributes greatly to the behavior exhibited at school, but whether a student continues to exhibit behavior in the classroom that was learned elsewhere is largely under the control of the teacher. After all, the teacher and the school are a part of the environment too. If other environmental forces can influence a student, why not the school? Educators who are willing to take an active role in effecting change can help students learn new behaviors regardless of the etiology of the problem behaviors.

One of the best ways of debunking the idea that there is nothing the teacher can do is to review available classroom management systems and then select a system(s) that is appropriate for the situation. The teacher can then list all the ways that a particular system might be beneficial to the students. For example, the reality therapy approach of William Glasser (1969) provides many ideas that encourage students to develop self-discipline. Behavior modification systems also provide an array of strategies that can be used in regular and special classrooms. Indeed, the proven effectiveness of these and other approaches should go a long way to dispel the notion that there is nothing that can be done. We'll have more to say later about specific strategies that could prove helpful.

Beliefs about Personal Control

The teacher who believes "What happens in my classroom is a function of forces beyond my control" is exhibiting what psychologists call an "external locus of control" (Levenson, 1974). People with an external orientation often attribute their misfortunes to chance or to the actions of powerful others. Louise's earlier comments about having bad luck reflect an external orientation. Conversely, teachers who believe they are in charge of their lives and what happens in their classrooms possess an "internal locus of control." People operating from an internal locus of control may also possess high perceptions of self-efficacy. That is, in addition to seeing themselves as being in control, they may see themselves as being capable of reaching desired goals. More will be said about self-efficacy in Chapter 2. Actions, or inactions, are closely linked to personal beliefs.

Teachers can benefit from an internal locus of control. Researchers (Halpin, Harris, & Halpin, 1985), for example, have found that teachers who feel in control of classroom events report less stress than teachers who see events as outside their control. Halpin and her colleagues note that teachers with an internal locus of control, believing themselves influential, take steps necessary to reach educational goals, whereas teachers with an external locus of control do not perceive the value of their own efforts.

Another benefit of an internal orientation is improved teacher effectiveness. For example, researchers (Sadowski, Blackwell, & Willard, 1985) have found that student teachers with an internal orientation are more effective than their externally-oriented counterparts. Specifically, the internally-oriented student teachers performed better in areas associated with motivation and classroom management.

Movement toward a higher internal locus of control is possible. Williams and Long (1983) suggest that a shift from external to internal locus of control evolves from successfully completing self-change activities. In brief, success on a given undertaking seems to foster the belief that you can control your life. Sadowski et al. (1985) also say that greater internality can be achieved by learning techniques that focus on teachers' influence on student behaviors.

Perhaps you have already identified a goal that could enhance your own perception of personal control. If not, one of the following goals might arouse your interests:

- Expand your knowledge in a teaching specialty.
- Learn more about strategies to enhance student motivation.
- Become actively involved in a professional organization that promotes teachers' well-being.
- Identify strategies for involving parents in classroom activities.
- Develop procedures to help students achieve greater self-responsibility.
- Work more closely with other school personnel.
- Plan visits to other schools.

What Lies Ahead

Given this initial attention to stress, myths about teaching, and personal control, you may be wondering if there are not more dilemmas in teaching than there are rewards. Additionally, you are undoubtedly aware that teaching has changed dramatically over the past 20 years. Family issues such as divorce, homeless children, and children in foster-care programs have increased significantly. Teachers in urban schools also recognize that they must develop a special understanding for working with students from minority populations who often come from a wide range of socioeconomic backgrounds. While there is reason for concern, the situation is far from hopeless. Teaching has many rewards. One survey of 2,000 teachers (''American Teachers Speak,'' 1984–1985) reveal that 96 percent of the teachers agreed with the statement ''I love teaching.'' Love of teaching is probably the most powerful force keeping teachers on the job. Students are also a great source of satisfaction.

Furthermore, students generally like school and their teachers. One survey (Clark, 1987) of 1,712 high-school seniors indicated that most of the students viewed their teachers as competent and knowledgeable. When asked to grade their teachers, 26 percent gave their teachers an "A" and 48 percent gave them a "B."

Besides the inherent rewards that accompany teaching, there are also many ways to improve those circumstances that might otherwise diminish the joy of one's work. Daniel L. Duke and Vernon F. Jones (1984), in reviewing the development of approaches to classroom management over a period of two decades, noted that, while teachers once had a problem with limited resources and knowledge of classroom management, now educators need help in coping with information overload. In sum, many resources to help teachers are available. This book is only one of the many resources that you might use. Each of the remaining chapters examines strategies that are oriented toward helping you determine your responsibility in managing various classroom activities; expanding your knowledge of techniques for motivating students and for managing inappropriate behavior; and for working effectively with students, parents, and colleagues in establishing better educational programs for each student.

Summary

All teachers will experience problems (or challenges). All teachers encounter students who are not learning to capacity. Most teachers also come into contact with disruptive students. But how devastating problems become depends largely on the way they are managed, and much of what teachers do with problems depends on the beliefs they hold about themselves and the circumstances confronting them. Teachers can benefit by examining how they view life and by trying to take greater charge of their lives. They can also benefit by working to teach students correct behavior and not merely trying to eliminate incorrect behavior. The joy of teaching is often a function of the positive things teachers do.

References

Abernathy, S., Manera, E., & Wright, R. E. (1985). What stresses student teachers most? *The Clearing House, 58*(8), 361–362.

American teachers speak. (1984–85). *Today's Education* [Annual Edition], *90.*

Besalel-Azrin, V., Azrin, N. H., & Armstrong, P. M. (1977). The student-oriented classroom: A method of improving student conduct and satisfaction. *Behavior Therapy, 8,* 193–204.

Burstall, C. (1978). The Matthew effect in the classroom. *Educational Research, 21,* 19–25.

Cheser, D. W., McDaniel, T. R., & Cheser, D. B. (1982, Oct/Nov). The effect of a classroom management course on teachers' disciplinary styles. *The High School Journal,* 1–6.

Clark, D. L. (1987). High school seniors react to their teachers and their schools. *Phi Delta Kappan, 68*(7), 503–509.

Duke, D. L., & Jones, V. F. (1984). Two decades of discipline—Assessing the development of an educational specialization. *Journal of Research and Development in Education, 17*(4), 25–35.

Feitler, F. C., & Tokar, E. (1982). Getting a handle on teacher stress: How bad is the problem? *Educational Leadership, 39*(6), 456–458.

Glasser, W. (1969). *Schools without failure.* New York: Harper & Row.

Gold, Y. (1985). Does teacher burnout begin with student teaching? *Education, 105*(3), 254–257.

Halpin, G., Harris, K., & Halpin, G. (1985). Teacher stress as related to locus of control, sex, and age. *Journal of Experimental Education, 53*(3), 136–140.

Kobasa, S. O. (1979). Stressful life events, personality, and health: An inquiry into hardiness. *Journal of Personality and Social Psychology, 37*(1), 1–11.

Lazarus, A., & Fay, A. (1975). *I can if I want to.* New York: William Morrow.

Levenson, H. (1974). Activism and powerful others: Distinctions within the concept of internal-external control. *Journal of Personality Assessment, 38,* 377–383.

McEnany, J. (1986). Teachers who don't burn out. *The Clearing House, 60*(2), 83–84.

Raschke, D. B., Dedrick, C. V., Strathe, M. I., & Hawkes, R. R. (1985). Teacher stress: The elementary teacher's perspective. *The Elementary School Journal, 85*(4), 559–564.

Sadowski, C. J., Blackwell, M., & Willard, J. L. (1985). Locus of control and student teacher performance. *Education, 105*(4), 391–393.

Sharp, J. J., & Forman, S. G. (1985). A comparison of two approaches to anxiety management for teachers. *Behavior Therapy, 16,* 370–383.

Webster, R. E., & Johnson, M. M. (1987). Teacher-student verbal communication patterns in regular and special classrooms. *Psychology in the Schools, 24,* 174–179.

Williams, R. L., & Long, J. D. (1983). *Toward a self-managed lifestyle* (3rd ed.). Boston: Houghton-Mifflin.

CHAPTER 2

For Better or Worse: Relationships in Teaching

"Roberta, that Cynthia Wilson is going to catch it from me."
"What's Cynthia done?"
"Before lunch I asked her to pick up the papers around her desk. She told me they weren't hers and that she wasn't picking them up."
"What did you do?"
"I picked them up myself and am I fed up. I've decided that I'm going back and give her a piece of my mind."
"Jan, do you think that's a good idea?"
"We'll see."

One of these teachers is about to make a bad incident worse. If the teacher gains anything from giving the student a "piece of her mind," it is likely to be only the temporary relief of frustration. What may happen is that her emotional reaction to one student could increase her propensity to respond emotionally in other taxing situations. And, if the teacher habitually responds in that manner, she could be perceived as a bitter person as well as one who lets other people control her actions.

People in all professions are faced with frustrations. Those frustrations often become either the basis for resentment or the basis for more effectiveness in managing interpersonal relationships. Few people remain unchanged by day-to-day experiences, and because the potential always exists for moving in unwanted directions, teachers must be especially conscious of the behavioral pattern they are developing. Teachers, of course, are not the only ones who should work at improving relationships. But in examining their own reactions to frustrations, teachers place themselves in a better position to help students act differently. This chapter, therefore, focuses on the teacher's role in enhancing relationships with others.

Affirming Oneself

Perhaps no factor has a more profound impact on influencing reactions toward others than the feelings that people hold about themselves. In fact, many psychologists contend that the feelings individuals have about themselves and others are inseparable. That is, individuals must feel good about themselves in order to respond positively toward others. Thus, initial efforts to improve interpersonal relationships should include procedures for establishing (or affirming) one's own worth. While there are many strategies that you might employ to affirm your own worth, we have chosen to emphasize: (a) believing in your potential; (b) speaking positively about yourself; (c) being optimistic; and (d) maintaining a balance in life. You can add other strategies as your studies and experiences reveal them to you.

Wanting What's Best

The philosopher scholar C. S. Lewis (1952) contends that self-love is basically wanting what is best for yourself. Similarly, loving others is wishing the best for them, too. While most people would argue that they always want the best for themselves and others, the acid test lies in their behavior. Their behavior should reflect wanting the best. You can apply the test to your own behavior. Do your actions build you up. Do they tear you down? If any aspect of your behavior does not contribute positively to your development, it can hardly be reflecting a desire for the best. What is your opinion? How would you measure self-love? Keep in mind that we are not talking about selfishness, but rather self-love or self-concern.

Believe in Your Potential

A fundamental ingredient in producing self-change is a belief that one has the capability to reach desired goals. Researchers (e.g., Bandura, 1977) refer to this belief as self-efficacy. Denham and Michael (1981) have linked what they refer to as "teacher sense of efficacy" (similar to the concept of self-efficacy) with improvements in academic performances and self-concepts; with willingness to innovate and to engage in professional activities, and with the desire to remain in teaching. In general, their review suggested that a sense of efficacy gives direction to behavior. In other words, people who think they can do something will likely do it.

Perceptions of self-efficacy are not limited to school life; feelings of efficacy may influence any aspect of living. O'Leary's (1985) review of research on self-efficacy and various facets of health, for example, suggests that perceptions of efficacy can affect motivation and reactions to a number of taxing situations. Among other health behavior, O'Leary reports that self-efficacy is related to the control of eating and weight, smoking cessation, management of pain, and adherence to preventive health programs. She also reviewed studies linking perceptions of efficacy to the control of anxiety, depression, and career choice and development.

"The magic has gone out of my module!"

Although a high perception of efficacy is a valuable attitude, the perception *alone* could result in minimal behavior change. Considerable effort is often required to change behavior, and with the best of efforts, setbacks can be expected. If setbacks occur, concentration on whatever successes can be achieved may be productive. A few possibilities for achieving more successes and a higher sense of efficacy might include: (a) associating with people who believe positively in themselves and others; (b) reviewing any personal and school-related accomplishments while focusing on the behaviors that led to those accomplishments; (c) establishing daily goals that allow gradual movement toward desired outcomes; and (d) becoming involved in school programs that improve your skills and knowledge.

Speak Positively about Yourself

The way teachers talk about themselves (verbally and nonverbally) can markedly influence how others react. Thus, appropriate changes in your self-statements can enhance your relationships with others. Because self-esteem is formed in part by one's self-statements, changes in self-statements can also be used to bolster self-esteem.

Those who are interested in eliminating negative self-thoughts or statements might begin by identifying positive alternatives that could be substituted for the negative ones. Positive thoughts about one's appearance, teaching abilities, and relationships with others are a good starting point. Listing these thoughts on index cards and referring to them at convenient periods during each day is one approach. Referring to oneself more positively during conversations may also have a beneficial impact on self-esteem. Of course, teachers want to be discreet about what they say. There is a big difference between saying, "I was pleased with the lesson," and "I did better than anyone else could do." Being thought of as a braggart can create negative reactions and consequently lower self-esteem. All teachers can benefit by thinking and speaking positively about themselves, but they should avoid extremes.

Accepting an honest compliment from others without making self-deprecating statements is also an important component in building self-esteem and self-confidence. When one is paid a compliment, it is far better to acknowledge it by saying, "How nice of you to notice" than to reject the compliment with a humble, "Oh, it was nothing." A willingness to accept the positive observations of others is part of the process of feeling better about oneself. Conversely, one can shut down any positive changes by well-intentioned rejection of kindness from others.

What's in a Thought?

Can teachers improve their self-esteem by altering what they say to themselves? A study by Hannum, Thoresen, and Hubbard (1974) suggests that they can. Hannum and his colleagues asked three elementary teachers who had complained of being excessively critical of themselves to alter their self-thoughts. The experiment began with the teachers using wrist counters to record their positive and negative self-thoughts during a specified hour each day. Positive self-thoughts included statements such as "I'm patient with children," while negative self-thoughts were revealed in statements like "I'm just too old for teaching." Subsequently, the teachers tried increasing the number of positive self-thoughts by cuing themselves to think a positive self-thought every time they engaged in a high-probability behavior such as looking at the clock. All three teachers were successful: positive self-thoughts increased along with a decrease in negative self-thoughts. Not only did their thinking change, but two of the three teachers reported feeling much more positively toward themselves. They said the experiment was among the most significant events in their lives. Unfortunately, the changes in feelings failed to produce immediate changes in the way the teachers responded to students. A follow-up interview, however, indicated that positive overt behavior changes had occurred.

Be Optimistic

How successful a teacher becomes could depend in part on the teacher's general outlook on life. Scheier and Carver (1985) contend that optimistic people — those who generally expect good things to happen — are more likely than less-optimistic people to achieve their goals. Scheier and Carver theorize that optimists will try to overcome obstacles when confronted with impediments to goal attainment, whereas pessimists are more likely to cease striving because pessimists have less favorable views about things turning out well. Scheier and Carver's research has shown that individuals who score high on their optimism scale also score higher on measures of self-esteem and lower on measures of hopelessness, depression, perceived stress, and social anxiety than those who are pessimistic. Further, their research has shown that optimistic undergraduates report fewer physical symptoms during the final four hectic weeks of a semester than less-optimistic peers. Scheier and Carver reasoned that optimistic students may be more persistent, may work harder at reaching their academic goals, or may take steps to deal with problems before they become too burdensome.

This might be an appropriate time for you to consider your own general outlook. Do you believe that most situations will turn out in your favor? Do you strive to produce desired results before circumstances get out of hand? If you could not answer these questions positively, you might try substituting positive forecasts for those in which you predict bad outcomes. Planning ahead is also a useful tactic. Further, acting in a more enthusiastic manner, greeting others with a smile, and keeping a list of all the good things that happen could lead to greater optimism. In sum, most people can probably benefit by avoiding the habit of describing their circumstances negatively.

Are You Happy?

One researcher (Fordyce, 1977, 1983) has suggested that placing happiness as a top priority and working actively at achieving happiness are keys to increasing it. In a series of seven studies, Fordyce has found that the vast majority of his community college students who chose to use the happiness information in his lectures reported increases in happiness as indicated by their mood states and changes in behavior. Among the suggested strategies that Fordyce's students found especially helpful were: stopping worry (which included keeping records and analyzing how few worries actually come true and substituting other thoughts for worries); being themselves; spending more time socializing; and developing more optimistic thinking. Other strategies included in his lectures were staying busy, getting organized and planning ahead, and forming close relationships, to name a few.

Maintain a Balance

Many teachers report that having interests outside of school facilitates the development and maintenance of total well-being. Williams and Long (1983), for example, say that a balance in work, health, social, and leisure activities is essential to personal and professional development. They note that the impact of too much or too little attention to any one area can spill over into other areas to produce grave consequences. For instance, the person who works day and night on school assignments can destroy family life or important relationships. The teacher who relies solely on work for a sense of personal worth may act resentfully toward students and colleagues who fail to be equally committed to the pursuit of teaching. In fact, any negative experience on the job could have far-reaching impact because the job *is* that person's life.

No exact formula is available regarding the amount of time one should devote to work versus outside pursuits. What is required for a healthy balance will vary from person to person. We suggest that those who are experiencing dissatisfaction with life examine whether too much time is spent in a single pursuit. Those who find that they are spending most of their time in work (study), might try to identify other activities that could be enjoyable. Swimming, jogging, or cycling are good health-related activities for many people. Listening to music or attending art and cultural events could also be potential leisure pursuits. And, of course, spending time with family and friends is an important consideration in developing one's social life. Establishing time, each day, to pursue activities outside of school helps to insure that one is developing a better balance in life.

Among the wealth of leisure activities, physical exercise may offer some additional advantages. Dr. Kenneth Cooper (1982), originator of the concept of ''aerobic exercise'' (sustained activities that are good for cardiovascular conditioning), reports that a state of physical balance (or total well-being) is needed for present and future happiness. He says that this state of physical balance comes from aerobic exercise, a positive eating plan, and emotional equilibrium (arising from proper rest, exercise, and diet). Other benefits derived from achieving a state of physical balance are: (a) greater ability to handle job-related stress; (b) less depression; (c) more self-confidence; (d) better concentration at work; and (e) greater perseverance at work. According to this approach, overall satisfaction with life might well be the end result. Need we say more!

Maybe Tomorrow

Sue was a hard worker who planned to find time for leisure activities whenever she got "caught up." In college she kept postponing developing any hobbies because she wanted to devote most of her time to studying. She frequently vowed that as soon as she graduated she would start enjoying herself. After graduation, Sue found that her teaching job was just as engrossing as her studies had been. She continued to put off recreation until the summers, but in the summers Sue found herself taking graduate classes and preparing for school to reopen.

One day as Sue entered the teachers' lounge she heard a teacher talking about retirement. The teacher commented, "When I retire I think I'll take up golf. I've always thought I'd enjoy that." Sue knew then that she was not alone. She wondered how many people were putting off "fun" until a later date. She wondered if she would even make it until retirement. She resolved at that moment to make leisure activities an integral part of her life. Today she is enrolled in an afterschool recreation program and is learning to play tennis. Tomorrow, who knows?

Affirming the Worth of Others

After examining strategies for affirming your own worth, you may wish to look for ways to demonstrate your belief in others' worth. Affirming the worth of others might include listening to others, looking for their positive qualities, responding positively to others, and considering the frustrations of others. Again, our list is not inclusive. Our intention is primarily to offer suggestions that can help you generate your own ideas for improving interpersonal relationships. If you feel that you are already doing a good job in this area, try comparing our strategies with your own.

Listen to Others

Listening is a procedure that all teachers can use to improve their relationships with others. Basically, listening is helpful because it permits teachers to learn more about what others think and feel. It also communicates the teacher's concern for others which in turn makes others more receptive. Listening to others, of course, is not a passive process. Effective listeners get actively involved in what others say and they demonstrate empathy for the speaker.

Becoming actively involved in what others are saying often begins by recognizing that you have something in common with them. Anything from sharing a love of animals to sharing a love of trigonometry could prove helpful. If you have a pet, for example, you are more likely to listen actively when a student offers news about newborn puppies. Chances are you will ask how many, what breed, and what is planned for the puppies. If you are not careful, you may end up with one yourself. When you do not share a common interest, you may have to work harder at listening actively. When that is the case, paraphrasing and directly commenting on what the student has said is helpful. A good way to begin a paraphrase is "You are saying . . . " or "You are suggesting . . . "

Concern for people—apart from the words—also contributes to effective listening. Psychologists use the term "empathy" to indicate the quality of hearing beyond the words to the feelings of the speaker. In a broad sense, empathy means that you can put yourself in the other person's place and view the world from that position. The empathic teacher stands in sharp contrast to the one who is unable to accept honest emotional expressions from students. The unempathic teacher might comment, "I am surprised at you" or "Don't you dare say that again." Such statements tend to cut off communication. The empathic teacher increases communication by responding to the feelings behind a student's words or actions. For example, the teacher may comment, "Carmen, you feel like you may have been mistreated," "Li, you seem upset by the discussion," "Richard, you act as though you would rather be working on another project," or "Gretchen, you seem very concerned about your performance." These and similar statements can increase open communications, correct errors in teacher comprehension, and help students recognize what they are communicating to others.

Students who recognize what they are feeling may desire to change. If their feelings are never brought into the open, they may never have the opportunity for complete self-awareness. Rogers (1969) reminds us that the empathic teacher is trying to communicate an understanding of student feelings, not to judge, evaluate, justify behavior, or prohibit expressions of emotions. Finally, a study by Waxman (1983) suggests that teacher empathy can enhance students' self-concepts and academic motivations.

We also add that an empathic listener is different from the sympathetic one. A sympathetic listener might cry with someone, whereas the empathic one is able to maintain the objectivity needed to be of assistance.

Project, Anyone?

How much listening are you doing? Do you put aside what you are doing when others want to talk? Do you avoid interrupting others? Do you comment on what others say, or do you switch conversations to what you want to talk about? Are you attentive to the feelings that words and nonverbal behaviors convey? Do you really hear what others are saying, or do you spend your listening time thinking of what you wish to say next?

To improve your own listening ability, you might record the amount of time you spend talking versus listening to others. A stopwatch could be used for documentation. Our college students who have done this have generally been surprised by the amount of talking they do. If you try the strategy and obtain similar results, you might enlist the aid of a friend to give you listening cues and provide feedback on the quality of your listening.

Look for the Positive Qualities of Others

Occasionally, teachers find themselves reacting negatively to a student. Such a situation may arise when the teacher is repeatedly confronted with disruptive behavior. It is not uncommon to hear teachers say, "He never does *anything* right." Of course, no student is totally bad. Even the most disruptive student will exhibit desired behavior in certain circumstances. Upon reflection, teachers must recognize that all students possess positive qualities. Thus, the goal of the caring teacher is to see beyond the student's disruptiveness to those behaviors that are commendable.

Many teachers find that they can focus on the positive qualities of their students by talking with them informally. Donna Oliver, a former National Teacher of the Year, says that she likes to stand at her classroom door and greet each student who enters (Long, 1987). She also uses that opportunity to say something positive to each student. Other desirable times for talking informally may be during lunch hours, before or after school, or at school social functions. These settings offer unique opportunities for getting to know more about students' interests, special talents, and needs. We frequently find that informal contacts with students give us much more positive attitudes toward students than can be acquired through classroom discussions where the emphasis is usually on academics. We do, however, have a word of caution. A few students may reject your initial efforts to get to know them better. More than one attempt is often needed to convince some students of your interest in them, but teachers who take a few minutes each day to talk with students usually find that students possess many positive qualities that would otherwise be overlooked.

Another procedure for identifying the positive qualities in students is to examine how student conduct is labeled. Once a negative label is attached to student behavior, it is often more difficult to see the good that exists. For example, thinking of any student as a troublemaker invariably inhibits seeing the student's virtues. Dropping derogatory labels altogether is a good strategy. Substituting a positive label for a negative one may also increase a teachers' awareness of the good in others. Referring to a student as "tenacious," for example, instead of "bullheaded" or "stubborn" could produce an entirely different opinion of that student. Similarly, seeing youngsters as "playful" rather than "rowdy" could lead to different perceptions.

Respond More Positively to Others

At least a part of the way teachers respond to students is a function of how students respond to teachers. Research in classroom settings (Polvistok & Greer, 1977; Sherman & Cormier, 1974) has shown that student behavior has a predictable influence on teacher behavior. The evidence from these studies indicates that when students behave appropriately (e.g., are attentive, follow directions, are less critical of the teacher), the teacher is more positive (e.g., praising). Conversely, when students disrupt learning activities, the teacher is more critical and reprimanding. Thomas L. Good's (1982) research summary also suggests that what teachers initially get from students may be a function of what the teacher is expecting.

Students' reactions toward teachers are changeable. The principle of reciprocal liking appears to exist in most human relationships. That is, others like us to about the extent that we like them. Students respond more positively when responses to them have been positive, and they are likely to care less about teachers, and to be less responsive in their academic work, when teachers are disapproving. Thus, an important procedure for getting students to react positively toward teachers is for teachers to make a deliberate attempt to be more positive. One study (Nafpaktitis, Mayer, & Butterworth, 1985), for example, with 84 subject area teachers in the sixth through ninth grades showed that the lowest rates of teacher disapproval were associated with the highest rates of student on-task behavior. In fact, Nafpaktitis et al. found that teacher disapproval accounted for as much as 25 percent of the variance in student off-task behavior. We will have more to say about approval and disapproval in Chapter 4. The point here is that changes in students' reactions to teachers can be achieved by changing teacher behavior.

I Changed. Did You?

Although disruptive students often reduce their disruptive acts, teachers are not always quick to change how they feel about those students. For example, in one study (Lewin, Nelson, & Tollefson, 1983), each of 19 student teachers in an experimental group was asked to select a child who exhibited behavior that the student teacher would like to change. After implementing change strategies, the student teachers reported significant decreases in the disruptive behavior of the targeted children; however, the student teachers' attitudes toward the disruptive students did not change. That is, there was a tendency to reject the disruptive children before and after changes in the children's behavior. The researchers suggested that feedback from counselors or others may help teachers to be more objective in their responses to disruptive (or formerly disruptive) students. Certainly teachers want to recognize that their reactions to students are often based on perceptions rather than actual behavior.

Consider the Frustrations of Others

Much student misbehavior is related to the frustrations that students are experiencing. Problems at home or with peers, disappointments over a performance, or any number of other frustrations can lead students to misbehave. Even when a student openly expresses a dislike for the teacher, the student may have no animosity for the teacher. Therefore, teachers must avoid overreactions to misbehavior. A more productive approach, in terms of increasing positive student and teacher attitudes in the classroom, is to view student misbehavior as something that can be altered, and develop behavior change strategies aimed at helping students deal appropriately with frustrations.

Considering the frustrations of others, then, often means altering one's views about behavioral change goals. Inappropriate reactions need changing whereas students themselves need acceptance. The zeal to change undesirable behavior can sometimes lead to attempts to suppress the basic structure that supports appropriate behavior. To illustrate, a parent was recently overheard telling her young son, "I'm going to break you no matter how long it takes." She then grabbed the boy by the arm and whisked him away. The "breaking" process probably proceeded more earnestly when she got the boy outside the store.

References

Bandura, A. (1977). Self-efficacy: Toward a unifying theory of behavioral change. *Psychological Review, 84*(2), 191–215.

Cooper, K. H. (1982). *The aerobics program for total well-being*. New York: M. Evans.

Denham, C. H., & Michael, J. J. (1981). Teacher sense of efficacy: A definition of the construct and a model for further research. *Educational Research Quarterly, 6*(1), 39–59.

Fordyce, M. W. (1983). A program to increase happiness: Further studies. *Journal of Counseling Psychology, 30*(4), 483–489.

Fordyce, M. W. (1977). Development of a program to increase personal happiness. *Journal of Counseling Psychology, 24,* 511–521.

Good, T. L. (1982). How teachers' expectations affect results. *American Education, 18*(10), 25–32.

Hannum, J. W., Thoresen, C. E., & Hubbard, D. R., Jr. (1974). A behavioral study of self-esteem with elementary teachers. In M. J. Mahoney & C. E. Thoresen (Eds.), *Self-control: Power to the person*. Monterey, CA: Brooks/Cole.

Lewin, P., Nelson, R. E., & Tollefson, N. (1983). Teacher attitudes toward disruptive children. *Elementary School Guidance and Counseling, 17*(3), 188–193.

Lewis, C. S. (1952). *Mere Christianity*. New York: Macmillian.

Long, J. D. (1987). *An interview with Donna Oliver: 1987 national teacher of the year*. Unpublished manuscript, Appalachian State University, Boone, NC.

Nafpaktitis, M., Mayer, G. R., & Butterworth, T. (1985). Natural rates of teacher approval and disapproval and their relation to student behavior in intermediate school classrooms. *Journal of Educational Psychology, 77*(3), 362–367.

O'Leary, A. (1985). Self-efficacy and health. *Behavior Research and Therapy, 23*(4), 437–451.

Polvistok, S. R., & Greer, R. D. (1977). Remediation of mutually aversive interaction between a problem student and four teachers by training the student in reinforcement techniques. *Journal of Applied Behavior Analysis, 10,* 707–716.

Rogers, C. R. (1969). *Freedom to learn*. Columbus, OH: Charles E. Merrill.

Scheier, M. F., & Carver, C. S. (1985). Optimism, coping, and health: Assessment and implications of generalized outcome expectancies. *Health Psychology, 4*(3), 219–247.

Sherman, T. M., & Cormier, W. H. (1974). An investigation of the influence of student behavior on teacher behavior. *Journal of Applied Behavior Analysis, 7,* 11–21.

Waxman, H. C. (1983). Effect of teachers' empathy on students' motivation. *Psychological Reports, 53,* 489–490.

Williams, R. L., & Long, J. D. (1983). *Toward a self-managed life style* (3rd ed.). Boston: Houghton-Mifflin.

CHAPTER 3

Getting What's Best: Prompting Desired Behavior

"I've heard that one of the keys to becoming an effective teacher is to get students involved in productive behavior. Do you think that's true, Bill?"

"I guess so. But I'm not sure that is the* only *avenue to success."

"I didn't mean it was the only thing teachers should do. But you've got to start somewhere. After all, couldn't we eliminate a lot of problems by first concentrating on what students should be doing rather than on what they are not supposed to do? Do you see what I mean?"

Bill is missing the point. If you can get students engaged in productive academic and social behavior, many of the problems that might otherwise occur will often take care of themselves. Therefore, this chapter focuses on ways for prompting desired student behavior. Specific strategies are discussed under the broad headings of: developing priorities; refining and communicating your emphasis; enhancing the learning environment; modeling important processes; and monitoring progress. The need to provide sufficient reinforcement for student achievements is also discussed. There are many issues that concern teachers that are not addressed in this chapter. However, the strategies that we have chosen are basic and should fit within the parameters of most approaches to classroom management.

Developing Priorities

A new teacher, and even an experienced teacher, has perplexing questions to answer at the beginning of the school year. Perhaps the most fundamental question is: Where do I begin? Although there are many plausible starting points, the most logical beginning is to develop broad priorities regarding what is to be emphasized in the classroom. We think there are a number of benefits to developing priorities early on. First, knowing what you want to emphasize should save time and energy. Commonly, when teachers become immersed in classroom activities, they find themselves moving from one activity to another with little opportunity to think about the importance of what they are doing. Developing priorities may help reduce irrelevant actions.

Second, developing priorities should help in maintaining your commitment to the curriculum plan if your initial efforts are met with student resistance. It is highly unlikely that commitment can be maintained without an overall view of what you are trying to achieve. Finally, developing priorities for managing the classroom can serve as a viable method for selecting and evaluating the worth of specific classroom management techniques. Often you may find that what you want to achieve is appropriate but that your techniques are unsuited to your situation.

There are many ways that you might go about developing priorities for your classroom. For example, it is beneficial to talk with teachers who are known to be successful in your field. You could begin by asking the teachers to identify important outcomes that they are trying to produce in their classrooms. At this point, you are not so much concerned with the techniques that they are using as you are with what they are trying to achieve. Successful teachers will probably reveal that they place a strong emphasis on promoting academic success, cooperation and good will, positive self-images, and movement toward self-discipline and a sense of personal responsibility.

Perusing research literature to assess what is being emphasized in successful schools and classrooms is yet another method for developing classroom priorities. For example, a recent review of research findings (*What Works,* 1986) indicates that academic achievement and rewarding success are the first priorities in effective schools. These schools also emphasize good conduct and work at establishing fair discipline policies. Other research (Williams, 1987) suggests that the most effective teachers stress positive reinforcement for appropriate academic and social behavior. In these classes, students learn that appropriate behavior is important and that it produces benefits.

After your initial investigation, your next step would be to make a list of the important outcomes that you would like to achieve. Of course, you will want to include any outcomes that are expressly emphasized as a part of your school's overall program. Possible broad categories might be: to develop feelings of self-worth in each student; to improve each student's academic and social skills; to help students feel comfortable in approaching academic tasks; to develop respect for the rights and feelings of others; to foster creativity; to encourage effort; and to provide tasks that will challenge each student to reach his or her full potential.

Refining and Communicating Your Emphasis

Although establishing priorities for your classroom will give you a broad perspective about what you want to achieve, you will need to refine your priorities to insure that you and your students have a clear idea of what is to be done on a daily basis. Such clarification can probably be achieved by establishing three widely recommended classroom management strategies: goals; rules; and procedures. Essentially, goals let students know what they should do at any given time. Rules serve as guides for desired behavior and pinpoint behavior that interferes with the learning process. Procedures indicate to students how they are to move from one activity to the next. Because successful classroom teachers and many researchers consider these to be important elements of classroom management, let's look at how you might go about implementing each of these strategies.

Setting Goals

Goals are the principal means of converting what you want to achieve into an approach that can be followed on a daily basis. All goals, however, are not equally effective in producing desired outcomes. In an extensive review of the literature, Locke, Shaw, Saari, and Latham (1981) found that goal setting is most likely to enhance performance when goals are specific and challenging (assuming that the individuals involved have the abilities to perform the tasks). These researchers also noted that task performance is enhanced when individuals accept the goals that are assigned.

Make goals specific. The most definitive conclusion in Locke et al.'s (1981) review was that specific challenging goals led to higher performances than no goals or vague goals such as "do your best." Thus, you will need to be quite specific in establishing goals for your students. One way of doing this is to state goals in quantifiable or measurable terms. For example, the goal of helping Lucielle to become a better speller could be made quantifiable by restating it as a goal to spell correctly 19 of 20 words on the next spelling test. Similarly, a measurable goal in language arts might be that students will be able to correctly state the main idea of a paragraph or a group of paragraphs. Obviously, the clearer that a goal is stated the more direction the student will have in knowing what is to be done.

Another way to make goals specific is to write down exactly what you expect students to achieve. Elementary teachers could list goals on the board whereas teachers in the higher grades might want to provide a

"I'm sorry, Debbie, but this isn't that kind of make-up test."

written list for the students or have the students write down the goals themselves. The benefits of this approach are substantiated in the work of Alan Lakein (1973), a leading authority on time management. Lakein says that successful people are much more likely to use written "to do" lists than are less successful people. He suggests that you write down everything you wish to accomplish, especially those things that otherwise might not get done. Lakein also recommends that you prioritize your goals and work first on the most significant items.

Make goals challenging. Goals can be converted into quantifiable terms yet still be inappropriate. For example, goals that are too difficult may alienate some students, and goals that are too easy will offer little motivation. Determining what are appropriately challenging goals requires experimentation. Thomas L. Good (1982) suggests that teachers may demand less from low achievers than from high achievers. For example, they may accept low quality or even incorrect responses from low achievers. Goals that offer opportunities for growth must be extended to each student and should enhance improvements in academic and social behavior.

One practical way to establish a challenging goal is to set the goal slightly higher than the student's present level of performance. When the initial goal has been met, new goals should be set. A student who knows none of the multiplication table, for example, might initially have a goal of learning to multiply the numbers one through ten by two. When that goal has been reached, he or she could be asked to learn to multiply by three, then four, and so on. Setting a reasonable time frame within which to master the multiplication table would also offer a challenge.

About Perfectionism

Are you a perfectionist? Individuals who set extremely high standards for themselves often fall into this category. David D. Burns (1980) observes that, contrary to popular opinion, perfectionists often accomplish less than those who set more realistic standards. Perfectionists have difficulty succeeding because they are never quite satisfied with their efforts. They will work and rework a project with the unrealistic goal of flawlessness. Additionally, when perfectionists do make a mistake, they often perceive themselves as failures.

Burns's idea of perfectionism does not necessarily include people who want to make improvements by establishing standards of excellence. His definition describes people who value themselves only in terms of what they can achieve and who will accept nothing less than a flawless performance. Obviously, goal setting is not intended to create the notion that anyone can or should be perfect. Nor is it intended to make students feel that they are worthwhile only when they meet certain standards. Goals should be realistic, and students and teachers should have fun as they work together toward common aims.

Encourage commitment to goals. One way to foster student commitment is to involve students in setting their own goals. However, be aware that students cannot always develop appropriate goals, especially for activities that are new to them. For example, Lee and Edwards (1984) found that teacher-assigned goals led to more overall performance gains on tennis skills tasks than did student-set goals. Both the teacher-assigned and student-set goals, however, were superior to general "do your best" goals. Lee and Edwards reasoned that goal setting may have posed difficulties for the students (fifth graders) who had never received prior instruction in tennis. On the other hand, student-set goals can promote student commitment when students are slowly introduced to goal setting. Kelley and Stokes (1984) found that student-set goals effectively maintained academic productivity for adolescents who had previous experience with student-teacher contracts. In these contracting experiences, the students negotiated work standards with the teacher and thereby began to develop goal-setting concepts.

Locke et al. (1981) suggest that supportiveness is vital to gain commitment and increase performances. In their review, they cite the work of Latham and Saari (1979) who say that supportiveness involves being friendly, obtaining others' opinions, encouraging others' questions, and asking rather than telling others what to do. So, when you initially involve your students in goal setting, begin by being as supportive as possible.

Developing Rules

A class discussion early in the school year is a logical starting point for developing class rules. Involving students in the decision-making process is especially important at the secondary-school level. However, even very young students can provide some ideas as to what makes a good or bad class. A modified form of the strategies presented by Taba (1966) for teaching cognitive skills could be used for conducting a class discussion to generate workable ideas for classroom rules. Initially, the procedure involves giving students a *focus* question (e.g., "What do you consider to be appropriate or inappropriate behavior in the classroom?"). After a student has responded, an extended or related question is asked (e.g., "Why do you feel that throwing erasers in the classroom is not appropriate?"). Students should be encouraged to explain and support their statements. For example, the teacher might say, "Juan, you state that we do not need a rule about coming to class on time. Give me some reasons why you think the class would operate better if we did not have such a rule." Ask students to predict what kind of classroom behavior will result if suggested ideas are or are not implemented. Students may have divergent opinions about some suggestions. All students should be encouraged to participate in the discussion and to defend their own beliefs about proposed rules (e.g., "Maggie, what do you think about the rule proposed by Juan?"). The discussion should generate student-developed rules that are acceptable to the teacher as well as the students.

Guidelines for establishing rules will vary depending on the ages of the students involved; however, a number of researchers (e.g., Madsen & Madsen, 1974) have provided suggestions for making rules that can be applied in most groups. Included among Madsen and Madsen's suggestions are: (a) involve students in establishing the rules; (b) keep the rules short and to the point; (c) state rules positively; and (d) periodically review the rules. Specific consequences should follow if rules are broken. Letting students know what is expected of them is critical to establish effective classroom discipline, but you would be naive to assume that rules will prevent all behavior problems. Whether students follow rules depends largely upon the benefits of rule compliance and the consequences of rule breaking. Madsen, Becker, and Thomas (1968) found that rules alone had no appreciable effect on inappropriate behavior. However, marked improvements occurred when rules were reinforced with teacher praise for appropriate behavior. Their studies also suggest that student behavior improves when teachers combine approval for appropriate behavior with ignoring minor acts of misconduct.

About School Rules and Policies

In addition to classroom rules, it is important that students know school regulations and policies that have a direct bearing on their conduct. Are certain school rooms off limits at certain times during the day? Is smoking permitted on school grounds? How many absences or times tardy are allowed before an attendance teacher is consulted? Questions of school policy are especially important for secondary-school students. Discuss regulations with students and post a copy in the classroom for continued reference to reduce rule infractions, provide each student with a small handbook or xeroxed copy of school policy, and take the time to discuss school policies during class periods. Stressing the positive aspects of school policies will increase the probability that students will stay within the rules. A discussion period will also allow students to vent any frustrations they might have toward certain restrictions. In cases where rules are felt to be unfair or unnecessary, help students work within the school structure to create change.

Developing Procedures

As with rules, discussions are a good way to develop and clarify class procedures. Students need to know early on how they are to do their work and what is expected of them as they move through the instructional process. For example, students need to know what they should do upon entering the classroom, when and how assignments are to be turned in, what is to be done upon completion of seatwork, how and from whom to get assistance when the teacher is busy. You might want to develop procedures for using the pencil sharpener, going to the restroom, studying in groups, and any number of other things that might have an impact on managing the classroom.

Besides clarifying procedures through discussions, teachers will also want to insure that students know how to carry out the procedures. In observing the beginning-of-the-year activities of 27 third grade teachers, Emmer, Evertson, and Anderson (1980) found that those teachers rated as more effective managers had a workable system for teaching procedures and rules. Both the effective and less effective managers initiated rules and talked about classroom procedures, but the effective managers expressed themselves more carefully and gave examples and reasons. The effective managers did not try to anticipate all situations: They emphasized most things students needed to know, such as use of the restroom, the water fountain, and the pencil sharpener. Time was spent going over the rules during the first several weeks. Some of the effective managers had students practice procedures such as lining up for lunch. Many taught students to respond to the bells and their call for attention. These managers did not jump into the basic academic activities that would later occupy most of their students' school day. They took the time first to develop procedures.

What Did You Say to Do?

Whether the teacher is specifying a rule, a classroom procedure, or giving academic instructions, precision is needed. Perhaps examining the following examples will help you communicate more clearly to your students.

UNCLEAR INSTRUCTIONS	CLEAR INSTRUCTIONS
Come in early in the morning and finish your chemistry test.	Come in at 7:45 A.M. and finish your chemistry test.
Show more team spirit.	Cooperate with team members by allowing other players to score rather than always attempting to run the ball. Show you are a team member by cheering others on.
Show you have some manners during lunch.	Use your napkin. Chew your food before swallowing.
Don't take too long in the bathroom.	You have five minutes to go to the bathroom before you board the bus.
Don't be so immature.	Spitwads are not to be thrown during Algebra II class. No note passing during discussions.
Don't get too far from the building during recess.	Stay on the asphalt area during recess.

In Review

Although no list of goals, rules, and procedures will guarantee appropriate behavior from every student at all times, clarifying what is expected from students should result in a more easily managed class. The following items provide a review of the major points that have been made regarding goals, rules, and procedures. They should be viewed as a starting place for any changes or additions you might want to make in developing your own approach:

- Establish quantifiable or measurable goals.
- Write down what students are expected to do and provide them with a list of the goals (on the chalkboard or in a written handout). If students are old enough, have them write out important goals.
- Establish goals that provide a challenge for students to move beyond their present level of performance.
- Encourage commitment by being supportive of student efforts in moving toward goal attainment or by having students participate in goal setting.
- Involve students in developing rules and procedures.
- Keep rules short and precise.
- State rules positively.
- Periodically review class rules.
- Establish rewards for compliance and consequences for noncompliance with rules.
- In addition to class rules, clarify school rules and policies.
- Develop clear procedures concerning how students are to perform any regular classroom activities.
- Provide students with opportunities to practice important procedures.

For more information on goals see Locke et al. (1981); on rules, see Madsen and Madsen (1974); and on procedures see Emmer et al. (1980).

Enhancing the Learning Environment

In addition to having a broad idea of what you want to emphasize in your classroom and a set of strategies for clarifying that emphasis, you will want to give considerable attention to creating a classroom environment that will facilitate learning. To do this, you should first answer two important questions: "What emotional environment is most beneficial for producing desired academic and social behavior?" and "How should I arrange the physical enviroment so that it is comfortable and encourages active student participation in the learning process?" Again, there are many specific things that you might do to create a wholesome emotional and physical environment. We will mention only a few of these to get you started thinking about the ways of creating an environment most appropriate for the individual needs and preferences of your students.

The Emotional Environment

The emotional environment of a classroom is largely determined by what the teacher decides is important and how the students are treated with regard to those choices. For example, the teacher who chooses (consciously or not) to focus on what students are doing wrong, ridicules them for their mistakes, and uses threats in an effort to maintain order will create an emotional environment that is threatening to students. In such an environment, students may be reluctant to challenge themselves for fear of making a mistake. Students may also be inclined to ridicule one another's mistakes.

Conversely, the teacher who stresses what students should learn and rewards their efforts is much more likely to foster a climate in which meaningful learning can occur. Many of the ideas presented in Chapter 2 about affirming the worth of others are related to the development of a wholesome and beneficial classroom environment. Another critical and important variable in developing a good emotional climate is letting students know that you are concerned about the issues that are of interest to them. One way of communicating this concern is to assess student interests and to use those interests in instructional activities.

You're Invited

In a positive approach to classroom discipline, Purkey and Strahan (1986) describe an emerging model for the teaching-learning process: invitational education. They believe that providing an inviting school environment for students acknowledges that students are partners in the educational process. They note that developing an invitational stance begins with trust *(involving students in decision-making and helping them learn to monitor their own behavior),* intentionality *(providing consistent purpose and direction that includes treating students as they can be rather than as they are),* respect *(positive attitudes toward self and others in everything that is done), and* optimism *(a positive vision that sees each person as valuable and capable). Purkey and Strahan also describe practices that create uninviting environments. For example, ridicule, sarcasm, and disrespect create an uncomfortable setting. If you are interested in learning more about the invitational approach, see Purkey and Novak (1984) and Wilson (1986).*

Assess student interests. Several strategies are available for determining what is appealing to students. For example, you might wish to develop a questionnaire to assess students' reading interests. Such a questionnaire could be designed simply to learn what types of reading materials students enjoy most. The questionnaire will probably reveal a diversity of reading interests as well as a few topics that everyone seems to enjoy. McKenna (1986) reports that young students tend to be interested in a wide range of materials. He also notes considerable differences in the reading preferences of boys and girls. But, in surveying the reading interests of 576 remedial junior-high and high-school students, McKenna found certain topics that seemed to have universal appeal. The students, for instance, shared an interest in "strange" topics. They liked weird but true stories and stories about ghosts, magic, and the unknown. McKenna speculated that books about oddities in science or a simple book of unusual math puzzles might encourage more reading in science and math. Similarly, reading about unusual events in any subject could heighten interest in that subject.

The class meeting is a strategy that William Glasser (1971a, 1971b) recommends for getting involved with students. We especially like class meetings because they are appropriate at any grade level, they reveal much about student interests, and they serve as a friendly basis for interaction between students and teachers. Furthermore, topics in class meetings can range from "What Makes a Good Friend?" to "How Can Math Be Made More Exciting?" Class meetings are similar to non-threatening discussions between friends who take turns speaking as they seek to share ideas on practical daily concerns. Essentially, the teacher's role is to guide discussion without passing judgment on what is right and wrong (as is too often the case in strictly academic discussions). If you don't like the ideas of class meetings or questionnaires, there are other strategies for assessing student interests. Observing students during their free time is one possibility. Whatever method you choose, learning more about students' interests will help you plan better for individual students and make them feel an important part of the learning environment.

The Physical Environment

The physical environment of the classroom may sound like a mundane topic, but the setting in which students learn could have a pronounced impact on their behavior and ability to learn. Something as simple as a variation in lighting, for example, can influence how students respond. Dunn, Krimsky, Murray, and Quinn (1985) report that students have strong preferences for either bright or dim light and that matching students with their preferences can promote achievement. Teachers can alter lighting by using bookcases, screens, plants, and other techniques. Dunn and her colleagues suggest that teachers encourage students to sit where they feel most comfortable. Of course, you would not want students to remain in dim light to the point that their eyes become fatigued, and you should insure that each student can see the chalkboard.

The seating arrangement can also be altered to improve student behavior. For instance, you might be interested in arranging desks to encourage discussions. If so, a circular arrangement will help. Rosenfield, Lambert , and Black (1983) found that, among fifth- and sixth-grade students, a circular seating arrangement was more effective in promoting student participation than were seats arranged in clusters or rows. However, if you prefer rows, there are still things that can be done to enhance participation. Weinstein (1981), in a review of research on the effects of the physical setting in the classroom, indicates that students sitting near the front and center tend to speak more freely than students seated in the back. Among other things, Weinstein suggests that teachers might increase overall student participation by moving around the room when possible, periodically changing students' seats, and encouraging students who typically select seats in the rear to choose seats nearer the front. Conversely, if you have a student who talks too much you might consider seating that student adjacent to you because being adjacent to the primary speaker tends to reduce participation.

A Little Elbow Room, Please!

Is it a good idea to bring students close together for demonstrations, reading sessions, and the like? That depends on how close the students come to one another. Teachers have long seen that placing students in crowded conditions generates pushing, shoving, and fighting. However, the desire to have students see material often leads teachers to ask students to "huddle around a little closer." Unfortunately, research indicates that crowding students not only increases aggressiveness but also markedly reduces attention to the teacher and the material. Krantz and Risley (1977), for example, found that asking kindergarten students to crowd around a teacher for a demonstration resulted in far less attention to the teacher and material and much more disruptiveness. Perhaps students become too preoccupied with their "personal space" to be attentive to lessons. Make sure that students have some elbow room when you bring them close together for a lesson.

The time of day that a lesson is taught could be another variable that influences how students behave. In an experiment involving students with short attention spans, Zagar and Bowers (1983) found that the students performed problem-solving tasks better in the morning and that they exhibited more off-task and noncompliant behavior in the afternoon. You cannot always control your schedule, but you can rearrange the time when you introduce some tasks. Less demanding tasks can be saved for the end of a class; students can occasionally receive breaks from a tedious task; and more time can be allotted for learning a difficult assignment. A little experimenting will reveal the best time for a particular activity.

Numerous other physical features within the classroom might be altered to insure that the classroom environment facilitates learning. You want to create an aesthetically attractive environment, uncrowded physical space, and an arrangement that minimizes traffic congestion. Also involve the students in whatever changes are made in the physical environment. Their involvement in making the environment an attractive and comfortable setting will help create a sense of "joint ownership." Students will behave more responsibly in a classroom that they have helped to create and partly "own."

Answering the following questions may help you think about the kind of changes that could be made.

- Is the temperature of the room comfortable?
- Are the walls decorated in a manner that generates student interest in learning activities?

- Do students have sufficient personal space? (Do some furnishings need to be removed?)
- Does the arrangement of the furniture minimize traffic congestion?
- Would changing the color of the room make it more attractive and appealing to you and your students?
- Is the room clean?
- Would changing the location of your desk facilitate observation of the students?
- Have you asked the students what can be done to improve the physical environment and have they been involved in implementing their suggestions?

Developing a Reinforcement Program

Another important component of classroom management is the formulation of a reinforcement program that will provide adequate rewards for student productivity. Of course, a great deal of reinforcement should come from students' successes as they move through the instructional program. However, students with a history of academic failure may not see success often enough to sustain their efforts. For these students, the teacher may find it useful to develop special systems (e.g., a token economy) in which students receive more tangible reinforcement for their academic accomplishments and appropriate conduct. We will give more attention to reinforcement in Chapter 4; the point here is that reinforcement should be viewed as an integral—and not a separate—component for promoting and maintaining desirable classroom behavior.

Modeling Important Processes

Another way to promote appropriate classroom behavior is for teachers to model what they expect from the students. Although teachers can model most desirable behavior, modeling is especially useful for demonstrating appropriate academic responses. After all, teachers are experts in their subject areas and students are generally inclined to follow the teacher's lead. Further, when students learn effective ways for approaching academic tasks, they are less likely to misbehave in order to avoid those tasks.

In modeling appropriate academic responses, it is especially important that teachers model the *processes* rather than the *products*. A classroom may be inundated with the teacher's accomplishments (as well as those of the students) and yet provide little information that will instruct the student how to generate those products. It is also important that teachers demonstrate that they enjoy what they do. Initially, humor and enthusiasm for the process may be more important than the work that is produced. Some risk taking and a willingness to accept a less-than-perfect product will encourage students to take risks and will foster a willingness to try. Because modeling academic responses often requires careful planning and demonstration, let's look at several research studies on how teachers have used role modeling effectively.

Combs (1987) has reported that poor readers often think of reading as a matter of identifying and calling words, whereas good readers view reading as a process of interacting with the text and constructing meaning from it. To determine whether role modeling would be effective in helping kindergarten students learn that reading is a thought process as well as a visual process, Combs compared role modeling with a more traditional approach to teaching reading: reading aloud to the students. When using the traditional approach, teachers introduced books by telling stories about the title and by making a brief comment about the content of the story. They held the books in such a manner that students could see the picture and the print. The teachers read with few pauses, and followed each book with questions about the contents.

With the modeling approach, teachers read from books with enlarged print. As with the traditional approach, the teachers emphasized enjoyment, but they introduced each modeled book by asking students to think about the story before it was read. For example, students were asked to speculate about what might happen if they were the character in the story. Teachers tracked the print with their fingers to model such concepts as the direction in which print moves and the idea that print conveys a message. The teachers also paused during the readings to "think aloud" about certain parts of the story, and they paused to let students confirm or disconfirm their own earlier ideas. At the end of each story, students were asked to recall important parts of the story and tell why those parts were important. The teachers often reread portions of the story to model how readers can confirm their ideas or make changes in them.

Combs's (1987) study revealed that comprehension and recall were much higher with the modeled approach than with the traditional approach. Students also showed more enthusiasm for the texts that were modeled, and they imitated (i.e., pretended to read) better from the texts that had been modeled. In brief, the modeling approach seemed to help the students understand that reading involves sight *and* thought.

Nist and Kirby (1986) have also used modeling and thinking aloud as an instructional tool in working with college students in developmental reading classes. They emphasize that although thinking aloud isn't a natural process it can be used to model typical thinking behaviors of active readers. A teacher can demonstrate thought processes by reading a paragraph and pausing to think aloud for students. Among other behavior, Nist and Kirby note that teachers can think aloud to help students formulate questions, make predictions, loop back to clarify a misunderstanding, and make connections between ideas. Nist and Kirby report the process to be particularly helpful in developing paragraph comprehension and study strategies.

What about Symbolic Models?

When the teacher serves as an effective role model, this is certainly a great advantage for the students. But there are other sources of effective role models that teachers can rely upon. Alvord and O'Leary's (1985) review of research literature, for example, indicates that films and videotapes are useful aids in teaching prosocial behavior. Their own research with nursery-kindergarten students suggests that human and cartoon characters in books and slides can also be used. Specifically, Alvord and O'Leary found that pictures in books and slides, along with audiotapes of stories, help teach nonsharing students to play with more than one child at a time, accept offers to join an activity, and take turns with toys. Can you think of any good books or slide presentations that might help your students develop a specific prosocial behavior? What about books that tell stories about effective interpersonal relations? Are there other ways that the teacher might use modeling?

Monitoring Your Progress

Whatever approach you select or techniques that you use in managing a classroom, you will need some strategies for monitoring your effectiveness. Essentially, progress in promoting desirable student behavior must be tied to the progress of the students. Several types of evidence can be helpful in assessing student progress. Among these are: feedback from students and their parents; teacher-made tests; and standardized tests.

Verbal feedback from students is an excellent beginning point in determining whether progress is occurring. Do students feel that they are learning in the targeted areas (for example, the areas that have been selected as major points of emphasis in the classroom)? The student's perception, accurate or not, is quite important. Students with a history of failure may perceive themselves as making little progress when objective data suggest otherwise. Therefore, it is important to identify inaccurate perceptions in order to work toward altering them. On the other hand, students may have a far more detailed, accurate picture of their progress than you do. They can point to events happening behind the scenes that more conventional modes of evaluation may not detect. If you are truly teaching skills that have applications outside the classroom, parents also may be able to verify whether their child is acquiring new skills.

A Suggestion Box for Students

Suggestion boxes are not often seen in public schools. However, in a classroom that maximizes student opportunities and responsibilities, a vehicle for achieving regular student input is imperative. An end-of-the-semester evaluation, like those that characterize college instruction, is insufficient for helping students who were enrolled that semester. An old-fashioned suggestion box permits students to give input while they can still benefit from it. You could invite students to suggest things they would like to do at school, resources they would like to have available to them, support they would like to have from the teacher, or things that are distressing to them about school. To make a suggestion system work you must be willing to protect student anonymity and implement some of the students' suggestions. A failure on either count will quickly erode the credibility of your system.

Probably the most systematic way of monitoring students' academic growth is with teacher-made tests that are criterion-referenced and with standardized tests. "Criterion-referenced" means that the student is attempting to reach a predefined mastery criterion as opposed to competing against other students. Ideally, you would have "pre" and "post" tests for the important goals that students are to attain. The students' progress over the course of the year can also be assessed in terms of performance on standardized achievement tests. Although we do not favor the use of these tests as the primary means of monitoring student progress, others may view this test data as critical evidence of student advancement. Consequently, you can hardly ignore the results. However, because the tests may not be tied directly to the skills taught in your class, and because some students may experience debilitating test anxiety during such tests or have special learning problems that render scores less meaningful, standardized tests often fail to provide a realistic picture of what your students have learned. We advise that you use such tests as gross indices of student progress and that you work toward incorporating the skills being tested into your instructional program.

Summary

One of the major distinctions between more and less successful teachers is the degree to which they anticipate and arrange what they want to happen in the classsroom. By defining in advance what they want to occur, successful teachers are able to minimize off-task behavior and help students develop the types of skills that can lead to greater success inside and outside the classroom. This chapter has recommended anticipating and encouraging desired student behavior by suggesting that you: (a) develop an overall emphasis (set priorities); (b) refine emphasis through the use of goals, rules, and procedures; (c) establish an environment that facilitates learning; (d) provide adequate reinforcement for progress; (e) model important skills; and (f) measure student progress. Of course, the suggestions offered here represent only the beginning point in successfully promoting student learning.

References

Alvord, M. K., & O'Leary, K. D. (1985). Teaching children to share through stories. *Psychology in the Schools, 22*(3), 323–330.

Burns, D. D. (1980). The perfectionist's script for self-defeat. *Psychology Today, 14*(4), 34–52.

Combs, M. (1987). Modeling the reading process with enlarged texts. *The Reading Teacher, 40*(4), 422–426.

Dunn, R., Krimsky, J. S., Murray, J. B., & Quinn, P. J. (1985). Light up their lives: A review of research on the effects of lighting on children's achievement and behavior. *Reading Teacher, 38*(9), 863–869.

Emmer, E. T., Evertson, C. M., & Anderson, L. M. (1980). Effective classroom management at the beginning of the school year. *The Elementary School Journal, 80*(5), 219–231.

Glasser, W. (1971a). Roles, goals, and failure. *Today's Education, 60*(1), 20–21, 62.

Glasser, W. (1971b). *Why class meetings*. Hollywood: Media Five.

Good, T. L. (1982). How teachers' expectations affect results. *American Education, 18*(10), 25–31.

Kelley, M. L., & Stokes, T. F. (1984). Student-teacher contracting with goal setting for maintenance. *Behavior Modification, 8*(2), 223–244.

Krantz, P., and Risley, T. R. (1977). Behavioral ecology in the classroom. In K. D. O'Leary & S. G. O'Leary (Eds.), *Classroom management: The successful use of behavior modification* (2nd ed.). New York: Pergamon Press.

Lakein, A. (1973). *How to get control of your time and your life*. New York: Signet, New American Library.

Latham, G. P., & Saari, L. M. (1979). Importance of supportive relationships in goal setting. *Journal of Applied Psychology, 64,* 151–156.

Lee, A. M., & Edwards, R. V. (1984). Assigned and self-selected goals as determinants of motor skill performance. *Education, 105*(1), 87–91.

Locke, E. A., Shaw, K. N., Saari, L. M., & Latham, G. P. (1981). Goal setting and task performance: 1969–1980. *Psychology Bulletin, 90*(1), 125–152.

Madsen, C. H., Jr., Becker, W. C., & Thomas, D. R. (1968). Rules, praise, and ignoring: Elements of elementary classroom control. *Journal of Applied Behavior Analysis, 1,* 139–150.

Madsen, C. H., Jr., & Madsen, C. K. (1974). *Teaching/discipline: A positive approach for educational development* (2nd ed.). Boston: Allyn and Bacon.

McKenna, M. C. (1986). Reading interests of remedial secondary school students. *Journal of Reading, 29*(4), 346–351.

Nist, S. L., and Kirby, K. (1986). Teaching comprehension and study strategies through modeling and thinking aloud. *Reading Research and Instruction, 25* (4), 254–264.

Purkey, W., & Novak, J. (1984). *Inviting school success: A self-concept approach to teaching and learning*. Belmont, CA: Wadsworth.

Purkey, W., & Strahan, J. (1986). *Positive discipline*. Columbus, OH: National Middle School Association.

Rosenfield, P., Lambert, N. M., & Black, A. (1986). Desk arrangement effects on pupil classroom behavior. *Journal of Educational Psychology, 77*(1), 101–108.

Taba, H. (1966). *Teaching strategies and cognitive functioning in elementary school children* (Cooperative Research Project No. 2404, United States Department of Health, Education, and Welfare). CA: San Francisco, State College.

Weinstein, C. S. (1981). Classroom design as an external condition for learning. *Educational Technology, 21*(8), 12–18.

What Works: Research about teaching and learning. (1986) Washington, D.C.: U.S. Department of Education.

Williams, R. L. (1987). Classroom management. In J. A. Glover & R. R. Ronning (Eds.), *Historical foundations of educational psychology*. New York: Plenum.

Wilson, J. (1986). *The invitational elementary school classroom*. Springfield, IL: Charles C. Thomas.

Zagar, R., & Bowers, N. D. (1983). The effect of time of day on problem solving and classroom behavior. *Psychology in the Schools, 20,* 337–345.

CHAPTER 4

Keep Up the Good Work: The Use of Positive Reinforcement

"Ted, I need to speak with you."

"About what, Mr. Solecki?"

"Your math homework. You haven't been turning it in. Why not?"

"I've been having trouble with the assignments."

"Well, let's review what you can do and maybe we can pinpoint the difficulty."

"That's fine. I could use some help."

The gains that are made by prompting students to engage in desired behavior (see Chapter 3) can be lost when students are not encouraged to continue with their efforts. Many students are successful in their initial efforts and receive a sense of satisfaction from their achievements, but others encounter difficulties and require additional support. For these students, you need to develop strategies to help them stick with an activity long enough for it to provide some positive benefits. This chapter offers suggestions for helping students continue worthwhile academic and social pursuits and to gain more enjoyment from school. More specifically, the chapter deals with the use of positive reinforcement to encourage desired behavior.

Defining the Limits of Positive Reinforcement

Like adults, students appreciate receiving encouragement for their efforts, and will work more diligently when they receive it. What constitutes sufficient encouragement varies from one individual to another. For some, good grades are sufficient while others need a pat on the back or a word of approval. When this kind of encouragement (or other positive stimuli) results in strengthening a particular behavior or skill, "positive reinforcement" has occurred. The good grades, approval, and so forth that are given to strengthen behavior are known as "positive reinforcers." Much of a teacher's work lies in identifying ways to reinforce (or encourage) students, for it is through positive reinforcement that achievements ranging from excellence in math to outstanding athletic ability are made.

Although positive reinforcement is a good way to encourage desirable behavior, researchers caution that with the use of positive reinforcement, teachers sometimes, unintentionally, support undesirable behavior. Positive reinforcement strengthens whatever behavior it follows. Teachers, therefore, must be careful to strengthen only that behavior that students should be exhibiting.

Did I Say Stand Up?

Have you ever known a student whose behavior seemed to get worse following criticism? One group of researchers (Madsen, Becker, Thomas, Koser, & Plager, 1968) who were interested in this phenomenon analyzed the reinforcing function of "sit down" commands. They asked teachers who were team teaching a group of 48 first graders to triple the frequency of commands to "sit down" to students who were out of their seats. Although the students usually obeyed immediately, the overall effect was a one-third increase in the time students were spending away from their seats. The researchers speculated that students will disobey more often when that is the only way they can get attention. Our story does have a happy ending, however. The teachers were able to reduce standing when they started praising students for staying in their seats.

No one is implying with this example that students should remain seated all the time. Our contention is that teachers should be aware of the potentially reinforcing influences of what they say and do. Also, teachers will find that directing positive attention toward behavior they want *is more productive than giving attention to what is* not wanted.

Reinforcing Important Priorities

In Chapter 3, we discussed the need for teachers to establish priorities for their classrooms so that they and their students would know what is important. To meet those priorities, teachers need to offer encouragement as students move toward these goals. More specifically, teachers should provide reinforcement for goal attainments, for adhering to school and classroom rules, and for following classroom procedures. Essentially, the teacher's responsibility is to strengthen behavior that benefits the student and is not being supported elsewhere. Ideally, your approach will concentrate on strengthening academic responses, but realistically, you can expect to invest additional time strengthening appropriate social behavior.

Behavior that requires encouragement from the teacher might range from school attendance and completion of assignments to participation in discussions and respect for others' opinions. What needs to be strengthened will vary from student to student and will depend upon the priorities you have chosen for your classroom. However, there is one skill that may require special reinforcing efforts: creativity. We mention creativity for several reasons: (a) creativity is often overlooked and even punished in some instances; (b) there is a need to recognize that reinforcement has broad applications; and (c) providing encouragement for novel approaches to problems will help many creative youngsters become more involved in group activities and dissuade them from engaging in disruptive behavior.

One way that teachers can promote creative thinking and problem solving (also a component of creativity) is to instruct students to be flexible and original in their responses. Because most students have learned to give the "right" answer, it may be difficult for them to perceive that it is all right to share their imaginative thoughts. Letting students know that unusual responses are both permissible and desirable should pave the way for increased originality in class. This is one of the many cases where telling students the conditions for receiving reinforcement in advance increases the likelihood that they will display the selected behavior (Maltzman, Bogartz, & Breger, 1958).

Glover and Gary (1976) have demonstrated that students can readily exhibit different facets of creativity when instructed to do so by the teacher. In their study, teachers systematically promoted different aspects of creativity (fluency, flexibility, elaboration, and originality) by simply writing one of these on the board and letting their students know that they would receive tangible rewards for displaying the featured behavior. Long and Williams (1982) also offer strategies for developing creativity, and you should refer to them if this area of education is of particular interest to you.

Using Student Preferences to Identify Reinforcers

Selecting reinforcers that will encourage students in any given classroom requires careful consideration. For instance, high-school students might be embarrassed by rewards that junior-high students find encouraging. Special education students may be uninterested in the reinforcers that improve the classroom behavior of regular students. What a person

"Mrs. Eggleston has been quite successful with reluctant readers."

perceives as reinforcing can also vary from time to time. Fortunately, there are several ways to find out what kinds of events, activities, and other sources of encouragement will meet the specific needs of your students: (a) observe your students during their free time; (b) ask them what they enjoy; and (c) use other resources, such as textbooks and research articles.

During free time, students naturally engage in activities that they most enjoy. Thus, observing students during their free moments at school will provide important clues about how to encourage their efforts in the classroom (Williams & Anandam, 1973). Observations might include making note of the books students read, the games they play, and the other activities that occur during their free time. Your observations will reveal that not all students engage in the same activities and that various options should be made available when a reinforcement program is implemented.

A second method for determining what will best serve as reinforcers is simply to ask the students. A class discussion can identify reinforcers that the teacher has failed to consider. A discussion is particularly useful with young students and those whose development precludes the use of written questions. Asking students, ''What are some things that we could do to make school more fun?''; ''What would be a nice reward for completing an assignment?''; and the like would be appropriate questions to include in the discussion.

With more advanced students, a written questionnaire can be used to find out what they prefer. Published reinforcement questionnaires are also available, but Donna Raschke (1981) suggests that teachers might wish to design and administer their own survey, using one of three questionnaire-type formats: (a) open-ended; (b) multiple choice; and (c) rank-order. With the open-ended format, students respond to questions about their preferences for free time activities, for seating arrangements, for ways of undertaking learning activities, and for ways of being complimented and receiving feedback on progress—to name a few. Among the examples that Raschke gives are: "If I had 10 minutes free time during this class, I would like most to . . . "; or "In this class, I feel proudest of myself when . . . " The multiple choice format is similar to the open-ended except that it permits students to select from a list of alternatives rather than having to generate their own list of reinforcers. Finally, the rank-order format requires students to arrange a list of items from high to low according to their desirability. For example, Raschke says students could rank-order the desirability of verbal approval, a food treat, a preferred activity, a sticker, money, a preferred item, a certificate of achievement, a pat on the back, and a display of their work.

Textbooks and articles dealing with classroom management may also yield ideas for possible ways to encourage students. Talks with teachers can add additional possibilities. Use what you learn to develop categories on different ways to encourage students. For example, *activities that encourage* might be one category. *Feedback* or *knowledge of results, praise,* and *special treats* might form additional categories. Positive notes to parents, approving nods, and asking students for their opinions might be listed under the *praise* category. Similarly, field trips, working on special projects, and class movies might fall under the *activities* category. You can continue to add to your list as you come across credible and appealing ideas.

Be Creative

A teacher's imagination and willingness to experiment are often instrumental in uncovering activities that turn students on to learning. Diana A. Mayer Demetrulias (1982) discovered that occasionally using cartoons in the classroom is an effective, and sometimes humorous, way for students to learn as well as to gain relief from standard approaches to vocabulary study. Her strategy involved having students use assigned vocabulary words to write new captions for cartoons and comic strips. Roberta F. Klumb (1985) has found that allowing students to act as peer tutors in a school-reading program is a good reward for improving classroom behavior, achievement, and self-confidence. If neither of these examples fit your situation, maybe you can come up with ideas of your own. What about games like "Jeopardy" to heighten interest in social studies and science? Or what about letting students have access to problems "for geniuses only" after they have done more basic problems first? Try to create some ideas of your own.

Minimizing Your Efforts

A legitimate and consistent concern of teachers is: How will I find the time to deliver reinforcement for desirable student behavior? You should develop a system for delivering reinforcement that fits within your classroom routine and that minimizes record keeping. Because teacher approval for desired behavior can fit within any class routine and requires minimal record keeping, it is the obvious choice. But some students may not respond to teacher approval and therefore may need other kinds of encouragement that take their preferences into account. One system that can be altered easily to suit the students and the teacher is a token economy.

Token economies have been used extensively with disadvantaged students. Kazdin (1982) notes that a token economy is essentially an economic system. The students earn, save, and buy, depending on how the teacher, the students, or both arrange and manage the economy. Typically, students work on academic and social skills to "earn" tokens (e.g., points, chips, paper money) that are saved until enough are accumulated to purchase back-up reinforcers. With the very young and with special education students, the back-ups are often small prizes and edibles; with other students, the back-ups are generally free-time activities. Teachers who implement token economies will want to provide a variety of back-up reinforcers to insure that something reinforcing is available for everyone.

You Can Bank on It

Jane Andrews (1981) is one creative teacher who developed a token program that helped students learn the value of money as well as good work behavior and academic skills. She did it with the aid of the "porcine paragon of savings": the piggy bank. Each day she allowed her kindergarten students to earn check marks for a variety of desirable behaviors, such as following directions and talking quietly. When a student accumulated 7 out of 10 possible checks, she or he received a play dollar that could be saved in a personal piggy bank that was made from construction paper. Read Andrews' article to learn how to make the bank and how the students spent their earnings.

If you teach "big" boys and girls, don't despair. We have a system for you, too. You can examine how play money was incorporated into a token program of rewards and fines to help a class of middle-school students make significant achievement gains in mathematics (Alschuler, 1969).

A "group contingency" plan is another reinforcement program. It consists of making reinforcement for *any* student contingent on desirable behavior from *every* student. Long and Williams (1977) found that group contingent reinforcers were as effective as individual reinforcers in improving classroom behavior. Group contingencies also seem to be easier to monitor than a system where feedback has to be given to each student. With a group contingency plan, the teacher awards tokens (e.g., points) based on the behavior of the entire class. Tokens are withheld from the class for the misbehavior of any student. Peer pressure operates to prompt misbehaving students to respond appropriately. The major pitfall to a group reinforcement program is that one or two students can "wreck" the system. The group contingency plan is also unappealing to those who prefer having each student rise or fall by individual merits. But for those who seek occasional relief from traditional approaches, a group contingency plan provides one means to encourage cooperative effort for group earned rewards.

Using Teacher Approval

Perhaps the behavior that most distinguishes outstanding teachers from others is their use of teacher approval of student behavior. For example, in a recent survey of 1987 State Teachers of the Year (Long, Long, & Williams, in press), the teachers were asked to respond to a number of questions regarding their priorities and instructional procedures. Although the responses to most questions were quite diverse and reflected the diversity of views among teachers in general, the responses to one question were very much the same. The question: "In what ways and to what degree do you use approval in your interactions with students?" revealed that practically all of the respondents ($N = 18$) saw themselves as making extensive use of approval. The following are selected examples of the responses made by these outstanding teachers:

> "If approval means positive reinforcement, I use it all the time and ask the children to reinforce each other. I teach parents how to reinforce their kids at home."
>
> "I use praise a great deal—even when I get a wrong answer. I might say 'well that's the best wrong answer I've heard today because it's sensibly wrong.' "
>
> "Being positive is how I like to be treated and so I treat my students accordingly."
>
> "All teachers need to respond *positively* to the student's correct answer or even to his efforts. All students should experience success before leaving the class for the day."

''Students' egos are fragile enough without teachers adding to the problem. Growth generally comes through approval.''

''I use approval a lot. I write personal notes on homework—notebooks that I require. I call home about good things. . . . I brag a lot, but I also am clear about my expectations—that I expect the best from the students I teach.''

''I always try to catch my students being right.''

''I smile, I nod, I hug, I pat, I hug some more, I sing, I dance, I inform, and I love my students. Most of all I listen.''

It is obvious from these comments that outstanding teachers share a strong commitment to approving their students and attempt to make approval a daily occurrence in their classrooms. Unfortunately, not every teacher uses approval extensively nor are they always successful in their use of approval.

How Much Is Enough?

In studying natural rates of approval and disapproval among 84 subject-area teachers in the sixth through ninth grades, Nafpaktitis, Mayer, and Butterworth (1985) found that the teachers averaged using appropriate approval about .90 times per minute and disapproval about .29 times per minute. Approval consisted of verbal praise, nonverbal approval (e.g., gestures, physical contact), and delivery of tokens or tangible rewards. Approval was deemed appropriate when it followed on-task behavior and inappropriate when it followed off-task or disruptive behavior. Disapproval consisted of criticism, isolation, fines, and penalties.

The natural rates of approval reported in Nafpaktitis et al.'s (1985) study were much higher than in earlier studies (e.g., Thomas, Presland, Grant, & Glynn, 1978; White, 1975), but the earlier studies looked only at the verbal behavior of teachers whereas Nafpaktitis et al. examined both teacher comments and nonverbal actions. The general conclusion of such studies are the same; however, approval and disapproval are very much related to the behavior students exhibit. Nafpaktitis et al. found, for example, that: (a) higher rates of appropriate teacher approval were associated with lower rates of student disruptiveness and off-task behavior; (b) higher rates of inappropriate teacher approval were associated with higher rates of disruptive behavior; and (c) higher rates of teacher disapproval were associated with higher rates of student disruptiveness and off-task behavior.

For teachers who expect on-task behavior of students to reach 80 percent or better, Nafpaktitis et al. (1985) suggest the teachers provide high rates of contingent approval coupled with low rates of disapproval. They say this could mean providing as many as 50 approval comments or gestures, 5 or fewer disapproval responses, and 9 or fewer inappropriate approval responses per class period. Although the approval figure may seem high, some teachers might need to change only the type of attention they are already giving. Of course, having the time and opportunity to provide high rates of approval could depend on the nature of classroom activities. We are not suggesting that teachers rely totally on any approach that might interfere with instructional processes. Combining approval with other approaches can also be effective.

One reason that teachers are sometimes unsuccessful in their use of praise, or approval, has to do with the inconsistency in its use. Brophy (1981), for example, says that few teachers consistently use praise for the purpose of shaping student behavior. He notes that teacher praise is often given because certain students know how to get rewards from the teacher or because the students possess personal characteristics the teacher likes. Thus, the praise offered is not part of any systematic effort to influence student actions. In brief, Brophy contends that only a portion of teacher praise actually serves as reinforcement. Brophy, however, does mention a number of other functions for teacher praise. For one thing, he says that effectively implemented praise can serve to encourage students who are experiencing feelings of failure and doubt. Brophy also notes that praise can reopen communication with alienated students, draw students' attention to their own accomplishments, and reflect teachers' admiration of student accomplishments.

The use of praise may also prove to be ineffective if it causes students to be ridiculed by their peers. This is most likely to happen when one or two students become the exclusive recipients of the teacher's praise. For example, public accolades that are directed consistently to the same students might result in their being called the teacher's pets. This does not mean, however, that a teacher should abandon using praise. Positive comments on homework assignments, gestures, winks, and private comments might be substituted for public pronouncements and serve to encourage continued good behavior. Additionally, teachers should insure that all students, not just a few, receive approval for their accomplishments.

Although approval is often used effectively, it is not always equally reinforcing. Adults and students alike will reject false praise. For example, we have all known people who use praise in an attempt to gain favor with those who are responsible for evaluating their job performance. The "praise" was offered to help the giver, not the receiver. This kind of deception is usually unsuccessful. Teachers who use praise solely to make themselves appear nice may also find themselves unsuccessful. Only when praise is appropriately used will it produce beneficial, long-lasting results. For this and other reasons, we are offering the following suggestions which are based on the ideas of Williams and Anandam (1973). Brophy (1981) also offers similar suggestions for using praise more effectively:

- Praise significant behavior. Students know when they have worked hard on a task and they know when they have expended little effort. Few students will welcome being praised on trivial matters. Observing and listening to students will enhance the chances of offering approval for significant behavior.
- Be precise. A student can be told that something is "great" or "very good" without much effort. Indicating what is particularly liked requires greater thought and attention. Perhaps that is why specific praise is more valued and less likely to sound insincere.
- Consider how you praise. One need not be grandiloquent. A wiser strategy is simply to make the approval commensurate with the student's actual performance.
- Use variety. Try identifying and using many different words, phrases, gestures, facial expressions, and forms of contact for conveying approval. Students may doubt the sincerity of a teacher who repeatedly uses only one form of approval.
- Develop consistency between verbal and nonverbal behavior. Telling a student "that's good work," while attending to something else, will not be nearly as effective as examining the work, looking at the student, and smiling while the approval is being given. Words may prove useless when nonverbal behavior contradicts what is being said.
- Try a gradual approach. Abruptly increasing the amount of approval can make a teacher appear awkward. Give students a chance to adjust to the new approach. Approval can be increased as students increase

their achievements. Other rewards can also be used in order to avoid overdoing the verbal approach.

- Encourage active participation in classroom dialogue. Involving students in two-way conversations communicates that the teacher is not trying to manipulate them. Students who actively participate in classroom interactional processes are also more likely to perceive praise as deserved (Morine-Dershimer, 1982). Thus, when praise is offered, it is likely to yield intended results.

General Considerations

Regardless of the approach that teachers take in encouraging student behavior, teachers should insure that what they are doing is both practical and humane. A practical program is one that can be incorporated easily into the classroom routine. A humane program is one that does not create unnecessary stress for the teacher or the students. Neither the teacher nor the students should feel "under pressure" about rewards. Programs that are intended to encourage should provide hope and enjoyment. The following questions will serve as a useful guide in your efforts to offer a suitable plan for your students. Any questions that cannot be answered affirmatively might serve as a basis for further evaluations and changes in the program.

- Does the program focus on behavior that is beneficial to the students?
- Is the program directed primarily at strengthening behavior that might not otherwise be strengthened?
- Have students been involved in the program's development?
- Are potential reinforcers available for all students?
- Do students understand what they are to do, and avoid doing, in order to earn reinforcers?
- Is the program easy to use? For example, can the teacher and/or the students easily maintain whatever records are required?
- Does the program avoid making the students dependent upon external rewards? That is, have plans been made to move students toward greater self-control?
- Does the plan encourage improvements in behavior?
- Are students comfortable in what they are doing?

Managing Difficult Situations

What has been said thus far is most applicable to students who readily display the behavior desired by their teachers. The student performs a specified behavior and the teacher provides encouragement to strengthen the student's appropriate response. A few students may seldom demonstrate the exact behavior teachers want. Thus, the teacher may encounter special difficulty in planning reinforcement for those students who possess few of the social and academic skills that can earn rewards. A technique known as shaping has been developed for enhancing the behavior of these students. In "shaping," responses are reinforced that resemble the desired response to some degree. A student response may include only a small component of the desired response, but by reinforcing small steps toward the desired response, that is, by requiring responses that are increasingly similar to the final goal before giving a reinforcer, the desired behavior is gradually achieved. Responses that have nothing to do with the final goal are not reinforced and are therefore eliminated.

The shaping procedure is often used in teaching academic behavior. Consider the method for teaching a child to print his name. For kindergartners and very slow students whose skills are limited to drawing a circle, a square, or a roughly drawn human, printing may be a formidable task. The task can appear more manageable if it is broken down into small steps that allow for frequent feedback and reinforcement. At the beginning of the process, a child's name is printed on ruled paper and the child is given the opportunity to trace over it many times. When the child is able to trace the letters accurately, he or she must more closely approximate the desired behavior by tracing letters that have been only faintly printed on the paper. Again, mastery of this step must be achieved before progressing to the next step: tracing the name over dotted-lines. Cues are eliminated until the final goal of printing the name without prompts is achieved. Prompting the response increases the probability that it will occur; fading the cues gradually increases the likelihood of a more independent response. In applied situations, fading and shaping procedures are often used simultaneously (Piper, 1974).

The use of the shaping procedure is not limited to developing academic responses. Social behavior, such as talking to others or volunteering in class, can also be changed using this process. For example, teachers often overlook the shy, withdrawn student who fails to participate in group activities. With more outgoing students clamoring for attention, the shy student may receive little or no reinforcement.

In shaping behavior toward a final goal of getting the student to volunteer to talk during class discussions, the first behavior to be reinforced would be one that has an element of the desired response. For example, you could reward the student for looking at you when he or she is asked a question. Asking the student to answer the question may result in further withdrawal. Instead, a comment such as, "I'm pleased to see that you are interested in the discussion," may be more effective. If you continue to reinforce only the initial behavior (the student looking at you), you will not achieve your final goal.

The next step will require rewarding behavior that more closely approximates self-initiated participation. For example, raising a hand to answer when a question is asked represents a second step toward volunteering, and should be reinforced. After the student begins answering direct questions, reinforcers can be given for comments that are not direct answers to questions, for example, "I'm pleased that you are sharing your thoughts on this matter." In this case, the shaping procedure would be continued until the student is comfortable participating in the classroom.

Reinforcement is a reciprocal process. As shy students become more outgoing, they receive more reinforcement and, as a result, increase participation. They also deliver more reinforcement, thus increasing the probability that others will be interested in interacting with them. The teacher can further prompt social interaction by arranging activities that require cooperative effort. Choosing an activity that a shy student can perform well, and naming that student as a group leader, may also facilitate the process. If, for example, a shy student is proficient in art, his or her group might be assigned responsibility for advertising a class play. The points to remember are simple: prompt the behavior and reinforce small steps toward the terminal goal.

In contrast to withdrawn students, hyperactive students are never overlooked. "He is like a whirlwind," "She never sits still for one minute," or "He's driving me up the wall" are comments often used to describe the child who is constantly talking and on the go in the classroom. Even though the behavior may rarely occur, hyperactive students can sit down. They can look at books. Desired behavior is in the repertoire of these children; it is just seldom performed.

To minimize hyperactive behavior, use of shaping is essential and the steps must be small. If the final goal is to teach a student to sit without talking and look at a book for 15 minutes, even one minute of the desired behavior might be too much to require as a first step. Perhaps 30 seconds would be more realistic. When the student has learned to sit still for 30 seconds, the length of time required before a reinforcer is delivered can be lengthened. The reinforcer for a hyperactive student will also need to be carefully chosen. Teacher praise alone may be insufficient reinforcement. Tokens that can later be traded in for a small prize may also be needed. To keep other students who are not being reinforced from getting jealous, the targeted student can be asked to share what is earned with the group.

Summary

This chapter has emphasized how to choose reinforcers for classroom use and how to incorporate those reinforcers into a positive reinforcement program. Special attention was also given to using teacher praise to your best advantage and to shaping behavior that is initially not responsive to standard reinforcement procedures. Throughout the chapter the theme has been to concentrate on what students should do rather than focus on what they should not do. Furthermore, our teacher friends say they are happier when they are emphasizing the good that they see around them.

References

Alschuler, A. S. (1969). The effects of classroom structure on achievement motivation and academic performance. *Educational Technology, 9,* 19–24.

Andrews, J. (1981). Banking on good behavior: An inventive way for children to learn while they earn. *Early Years, 11*(2), 52–54.

Brophy, J. (1981). On praising effectively. *The Elementary School Journal, 81* (5), 269–278.

Demetrulias, D. A. M. (1982). Gags, giffles, guffaws: Using cartoons in the classroom. *Journal of Reading, 26,* 66–68.

Glover, J., & Gary, A. (1976). Procedures to increase some aspects of creativity. *Journal of Applied Behavior Analysis, 9,* 79–84.

Kazdin, A. E. (1982). The token economy: A decade later. *Journal of Applied Behavior Analysis, 15,* 431–445.

Klumb, R. F. (1985). Peer tutoring is a reward. *The Reading Teacher, 39*(1), 115–116.

Long, E. W., Long, J. D., & Williams, R. L. (in press). Self-reported use of approval by outstanding teachers. *Education*.

Long, J. D., & Williams, R. L. (1977). The comparative effectiveness of group and individually contingent free time with inner-city junior high school students. In K. D. O'Leary & S. G. O'Leary (Eds.), *Classroom management: The successful use of behavior modification* (2nd ed). New York: Pergamon Press.

Long, J. D., & Williams, R. L. (1982). *SOS for teachers: Strategies of self-improvement*. Princeton, NJ: Princeton Book Co.

Madsen, C. H., Jr., Becker, W. C., Thomas, D. R., Koser, L., & Plager, E. (1968). An analysis of the reinforcing function of "sit down" commands. In R. K. Parker (Ed.), *Readings in educational psychology*. Boston: Allyn and Bacon.

Maltzman, I., Bogartz, W., & Breger, L. (1958). A procedure for increasing word association originality and its transfer effects. *Journal of Experimental Psychology, 56,* 392–398.

Morine-Dershimer, G. (1982). Pupil perceptions of teacher praise. *Elementary School Journal, 82,* 421–434.

Nafpaktitis, M., Mayer, G. R., & Butterworth, T. (1985). Natural rates of teacher approval and disapproval and their relation to student behavior in intermediate school classrooms. *Journal of Educational Psychology, 77*(3), 362–367.

Piper, T. (1974). *Classroom management and behavior objectives*. Belmont, CA: Lear Siegler/Fearon.

Raschke, D. (1981). Designing reinforcement surveys—Let students choose the reward. *Teaching Exceptional Children, 14,* 92–96.

Schunk, D. H. (1984). Enhancing self-efficacy and achievement through rewards and goals: Motivational and informational effects. *Journal of Educational Research, 78*(1), 29–34.

Thomas, J. D., Presland, I. E., Grant, M. D., & Glynn, T. (1978). Natural rates of teacher approval in grade 7 classrooms. *Journal of Applied Behavior Analysis, 11,* 91–94.

White, M. A. (1975). Natural rates of teacher approval and disapproval in the classroom. *Journal of Applied Behavior Analysis, 8,* 367–372.

Williams, R. L., & Anadam, K. (1973). *Cooperative classroom management*. Columbus, OH: Charles E. Merrill.

CHAPTER 5

In Pursuit of Harmony: Strategies for Managing Inappropriate Student Behavior

"Everybody's doing it. He's too busy grading papers to catch you."

"Everybody isn't cheating. And besides, even if he didn't catch me, I'm not sure it would get me anywhere."

"You're such a Puritan. Look, it got me higher grades."

"Yeh, but are you learning anything? I want to be an engineer someday."

"Me too, and good grades are going to help."

"Sure they will, but how about having to cross those bridges you build?"

Ultimately, inappropriate behavior does not pay. This is one of the important lessons to be learned in life. Unfortunately, many adults have learned that lesson the hard way. They have made mistakes and faced harsh consequences. Their sorrowful refrain is often, "If only someone had warned me." Of course, no one can be totally protected from the consequences of wrong decisions, but students can often be spared the bitter experiences that result from developing unacceptable behavior patterns.

The two preceding chapters have suggested that much inappropriate behavior can be prevented by fostering and rewarding the development of appropriate behavior. Nonetheless, students will occasionally engage in behavior that is not in their long-term best interests. Thus, teachers need to know acceptable strategies to control inappropriate behavior when it does occur. One way that teachers can increase their knowledge is to review the research literature to determine what techniques are recommended for coping with the challenges in today's classrooms.

Fortunately, a number of researchers have already conducted reviews that could be beneficial and timesaving for teachers. For example, Williams (1987) analyzed 186 research studies in classroom management research from 1980 through 1983 in mainstream journals on educational psychology, school psychology, and applied behavior analysis, and compiled strategies both for strengthening appropriate and for weakening inappropriate behavior. The most frequently reported strategies for curtailing inappropriate behavior included response cost procedures (reported in 14 studies), some form of reprimands (9 studies), some form of differential reinforcement (7 studies), and ignoring the behavior (4 studies). In this chapter, we will examine these as well as other strategies (e.g., timeout, natural and logical consequences, and feedback) that

"I don't like suspensions. Why give time off for bad behavior?"

could prove helpful in classroom management. We will begin by looking at informative feedback, a positive intervention strategy often used for increasing desired behavior but also useful for weakening inappropriate behavior. We will conclude by offering a few suggestions for choosing strategies for different classroom situations.

Informative Feedback

Some researchers (e.g., Lobitz & Burns, 1977) suggest that feedback may be the least intrusive intervention strategy. Teachers will want to give primary consideration to using feedback. Essentially, feedback (or knowledge of results) is presented in a neutral fashion, without praise or criticism, to provide individuals with information about their behavior. Most typically, feedback has been used as a motivational technique for attaining academic goals, but it also appears to be emerging as a means for managing classroom behavior problems. For example, in a statistical analysis of single-case studies that used reinforcement or feedback to manage behavior problems, Skiba, Casey, and Center (1985) found that feedback can be effective in reducing disruptive classroom behavior. These researchers noted, however, that there is difficulty in appraising the effectiveness of feedback. Reinforcement procedures include an informational component and many procedures that might legitimately be classified as feedback (e.g., self-recording) are often referred to in other ways.

Two early studies illustrate the effective use of feedback alone. Drabman and Lahey (1977) showed that the disruptive behavior of one student was reduced by having the teacher inform the child that the teacher was rating the child's behavior (a scale of 0 to 10 was used to indicate very poor to very good behavior) and subsequently quietly presenting the child with a total score based on those ratings. They emphasize, however, that the effects of feedback alone may be temporary if not combined with other strategies such as positive reinforcement. In a similar study, Lobitz and Burns (1977) found that revealing to the entire class how well a student was remaining on-task was more effective in reducing off-task behavior than talking to the child privately. But they indicate that the private feedback procedure did not include enough data points to give a stable picture of the behavior under that condition.

Other writers have also suggested that some form of feedback may be helpful in reducing misconduct. For example, Dreikurs has long advocated *corrective feedback* as a means of dealing with behavior problems (Dreikurs, Brunwald, & Pepper, 1971). As used by Dreikurs, "corrective feedback" is a means of heightening a student's awareness of the motives for misbehavior. The first step in using corrective feedback is to ask the student why he or she is misbehaving. If the student can state the motive, the student and teacher can proceed to identifying behavior that would be more useful for meeting the student's needs.

If the student cannot give the reason for the conduct, and few can, then the teacher should suggest the motive. For example, with a child who appears to be misbehaving to gain attention, the teacher might say, "Could it be that you feel the only way to be noticed is to misbehave?" The teacher who correctly suggests the student's motive will frequently elicit a *recognition reflex*. A "recognition reflex" can be a smile, an "ah-ha" expression, or other behavior that indicates, "You may have something there." Dreikurs suggests that the student may change as a result of the new awareness. This approach, of course, is different from behavioral approaches in that it deals with the presumed motives underlying behavior rather than concentrating primarily on behavior changes.

Our experience also suggests that many students do not have an accurate picture of how their behavior is being perceived by others. Informative feedback can be especially useful when students ask for advice. You might want to reserve feedback for such situations. Sometimes a complaint to the teacher is the student's indirect way of asking for advice. Also, a student may occasionally be straightforward and ask, "What do you think I am doing wrong?" or "Why don't others seem to like me?" Once the students has asked, the stage is set for candid feedback.

What If They Don't Ask?

Is unsolicited feedback helpful? In academic areas, information about progress or ways of making improvements may be welcomed—whether solicited or not—provided it is offered in a helpful, non-threatening manner. But teachers observe a good deal of problem behavior that is unrelated to academics. For example, many students have difficulty forming friendships. Many students also have irritating habits that generate negative reactions from others. In these and similar circumstances, should the teacher intervene and offer an opinion? Possibly. But if feedback is the strategy selected, the student should be approached with genuine concern. A possible starting point wuld be for the teacher to say something like, "I've noticed you are having difficulties with ... Would you like my reaction?" If learning activities are not being disrupted, students could be given the option of accepting or rejecting the offer of feedback. After all, other strategies (e.g., positive reinforcement, self-management projects, and other strategies described in this and other texts) do exist for enhancing interpersonal relations. Finally, if the student rejects the offer of feedback, the teacher should listen carefully as well as express a desire to help at any time.

Communicating clearly and candidly how you perceive a student's behavior is not always easy. Your views may initially be met with resistance or anger. If students refuse to accept your feedback, remain calm and keep the door to communication open. Students' first reactions may not represent the way they will react after having some time to think about what you have said. The following suggestions offered by Williams and Long (1983, p. 330) can help make feedback more acceptable to students:

- Offer feedback in a tentative rather than in an absolute manner. For example, you might say: "Is this a possibility?"; "Have you noticed ... ?"; or "I wonder if you have thought that ... ?"
- If the student becomes defensive, refrain from being defensive yourself. Stop talking and listen. You might comment: "You're surprised I'm saying this"; or "You're upset that I'm giving you this information." This approach could help the student understand that you sense frustration and may permit further feedback at a later time.
- Give precise feedback. Speak about how often you have observed the behavior rather than attacking the individual. For example, you might say: "I noticed you had three arguments today" rather than saying, "You're always arguing with somebody."
- If you pinpoint an inappropriate behavior, suggest how the student might improve that behavior. Tell the student about any improvement you have noticed.
- Try giving positive feedback in addition to any negative feedback. Always start and end on a positive point.

- Finally, we would add that feedback should be limited. Don't overpower students by bringing up past mistakes. Stick to the present and remember that unsolicited feedback on an array of indiscretions is likely to produce more resentment than change.

If you feel that you are informing students too frequently about how you see things, you might try using feedback in another way. For example, you can let students maintain records of their own behavior. This is helpful when students are old enough to count certain kinds of responses or measure the duration of a particular behavior. Students often gain useful insight by logging such things as how often they remain on or off task, get upset, interrupt others, make "cute" remarks, and the like. But whether you provide the insight or they record their own actions, the goal remains the same: to provide self-knowledge and subsequent behavioral improvement.

Differential Reinforcement

Various forms of differential reinforcement are also among the positive intervention strategies that teachers will want to consider for weakening inappropriate behavior. Two procedures that emerged in Williams' (1987) analysis of research trends were *differential reinforcement of low rate of responding* (DRL) and *differential reinforcement of other behaviors* (DRO). DRL involves reinforcing a student for exhibiting fewer and fewer instances of inappropriate behavior (Williams, 1987). Although similar to DRL, DRO involves the delivery of a reinforcer for the *absence* of a designated undesirable behavior (Poling & Ryan, 1982).

A common classroom strategy used in implementing DRO is to set a kitchen timer and reward those students who refrain from misbehaving during the timed interval. Gradually the time that students must refrain from misbehaving is increased. Poling and Ryan (1982) note, however, that having to reinforce students and reset a timer after short intervals may be time consuming for the teacher. Nonetheless, DRO may prove helpful when there is little desired behavior to reinforce. With DRO, students at least receive a reward for *not* misbehaving. And teachers can use the time when students do not misbehave to teach desired behavior that subsequently can be strengthened. Finally, Poling and Ryan's review shows that DRO is a widely used and effective strategy for weakening inappropriate behavior in the mentally retarded.

Another reinforcement procedure that did not emerge in Williams' (1987) review, but which is potentially useful for teachers, is the *differential reinforcement of incompatible behavior* (DRI). One behavior is said to be incompatible with another, or to compete with another, when they cannot occur simultaneously (Kazdin, 1984). For example, students cannot be tardy and punctual, talk and listen, or agree and disagree at the same time. Thus, when teachers are confronted with misconduct, the task is to identify and strengthen the opposite behavior. Teachers who are able to increase academic peformance are often able to report a decrease in classroom disruptiveness because academic performance and disruptiveness are generally incompatible.

A study by Ayllon and Roberts (1974) clearly demonstrates the benefits of reinforcing opposite responses. These researchers were interested in reducing negative behavior among five of the most disruptive students in a large fifth-grade reading class (38 students). The average level of disruptive behavior for these students was 34 percent. Not surprisingly, these students' correct responses on daily reading assignments was below 50 percent. The disruptive behavior included running, walking around the room, loud talking, noise-making, and a variety of other overt actions. Instead of trying to reduce the behavior directly through punishment and other means, a token economy was established. The system enabled students to earn points for completing academic assignments. Students could earn two points for 80 percent accuracy on an assignment and five points for 100 percent accuracy on an assignment. The points could be cashed in daily or weekly for a variety of backup reinforcers. For example, two points would buy 15 minutes access to a game room or 10 minutes of extra recess. Reduced detention, becoming an assistant teacher, and having free time to work on the bulletin board were a few of the other backup reinforcers that could be purchased.

The results of Ayllon and Roberts' (1974) study were highly encouraging. By the end of the study, the average rate of accuracy on academic performance for the five most disruptive students rose to about 85 percent. Although no direct effort had been made to reduce disruptiveness, the average rate of disruptive behavior fell to about 5 percent. Apparently, the kind of behavior being reinforced was incompatible with disruptiveness. Students were reportedly heard making such remarks as, "Shut up, I'm trying to do my work," and "Quit bugging me, can't you see I'm reading?" The usefulness of reinforcing responses that are incompatible with disruptiveness has also been documented by other researchers (e.g., Aaron & Bostow, 1978; Simon, Ayllon, & Milan, 1982).

Although DRI sounds easy to implement, difficulties may arise regarding the selection of appropriate behavior to reinforce. For example, a study by Kelly and Bushell (1987) suggests that differential reinforcement of students' hand raising to solicit teacher contact might prove counterproductive. In fact, Kelly and Bushell found that having teachers attend to students while they were on task produced more on-task behavior and achievement than did attention for hand raising following the completion of work. In other words, the time that students had their hands raised in order to have their work checked turned out to be incompatible with on-task behavior.

Reinforcing the wrong behavior may not be the only problem with using DRI. Reinforcing behavior in one setting but not in another could lead to increased unwanted behavior in the settings where no reinforcement is offered. This observation has been made in laboratory studies and has been documented in classroom research as well (Simon, Ayllon, & Milan, 1982). Increasing the number of places where teachers reinforce responses that compete with misbehavior, however, should reduce the likelihood of increases in unwanted responses. Furthermore, stressing appropriate behavior in a variety of settings will keep the focus on what students should be doing rather than diverting too much attention to what should not be done. Of course, any reinforcement that is offered for appropriate behavior must be greater than that received for inappropriate behavior; otherwise there is insufficient incentive for change.

Searching for Opposites

A good way to discourage misconduct is to promote responses that cannot exist simultaneously with poor conduct. Merely reinforcing a desired, but unrelated, response isn't likely to control specific problems. For example, reinforcing sharing is unlikely to reduce biting.

To gain practice in identifying opposites (incompatible responses) that you can reinforce, try working with a colleague. List troublesome misbehavior and then see if the two of you can identify legitimate opposites to strengthen. For example, what is the opposite of biting? (Hint: Can kindergarten students smile and bite simultaneously?) What about defiance? Lying? Kicking? Laughing at others' mistakes? Disagreeableness?

Ignoring Minor Infractions

Another nonpunitive technique for weakening inappropriate behavior is to ignore minor infractions. Studies (Madsen, Becker, & Thomas, 1968; Kindall, Workman, & Williams, 1980) suggest, however, that for this to be an effective strategy, it should be combined with praise for appropriate behavior. Of course, no one suggests that teachers ignore every deviant act that occurs. Ignoring certain infractions could be catastrophic. When students risk injury to themselves or others, for example, the teacher should respond quickly, but teachers should not make a game of trying to catch students in every indiscretion.

Ignoring some misconduct is a useful addition to classroom management, but teachers should know in advance what they will and will not overlook, and they need to follow through with their plans. Additionally, because peers can provide reinforcement for behavior that the teacher is trying to weaken, Craig, Mehrens, & Clarizio (1975) suggest that teachers enlist the cooperation of students in controlling behavior. This kind of cooperative approach is especially important when trying to deal with a class clown.

The Final Word

Manuel, a junior-high teacher, frequently found himself arguing with one of his students. The arguments typically started when the student would try to get in the last word after Manuel had corrected her or asked her to do something. One of Manuel's colleagues advised him to walk away after he had given instructions to the student. The colleague reasoned that the student would be deprived of reinforcement for talking back. Manuel didn't feel he should ignore any student remarks. What do you think? Is there a time to walk away? Is ignoring (or in this case, walking away) the same as pretending not to notice that a remark has been made?

Developing a Cooperative Approach

A class discussion can help students recognize the importance of peer approval and can gain their support in managing misconduct. During such a discussion, you might ask: "Why do some students break rules when it only gets them into trouble? What would happen if no one paid attention when these students engaged in disruptive activities? How can classmates help one another make academic progress?'' Most students will surmise that peer attention often sustains undesirable behavior and that withholding their attention could help these classmates. Students will understand that showing approval for appropriate behavior will have a positive impact on the entire class. Periodic discussions about peer approval will sharpen everyone's understanding about the variables that shape behavior and will lead to better self-understanding. Some disruptive youngsters might alter their behavior after understanding what influences their actions. Further, teachers can use these discussions to solicit cooperation from the class.

Teachers should avoid having discussions about disruptiveness immediately following an unpleasant classroom incident. Class discussions should not be used to embarrass students. A better approach is to select a time when students are well behaved to talk about disruptiveness. Discussions could be held when class rules are being established, or during the time set aside for discussing class activities with students. Establishing a cooperative planning time (for example, every grading period) to discuss classroom concerns is a good idea for teachers at all grade levels.

Of course, teachers should encourage students to use peer approval more judiciously. Teacher recognition is sufficient reinforcement for most students, but special privileges, tangibles, or tokens might also be considered. Long and Williams (1973) have shown that group rewards are also useful in getting students to control each others' behavior. When a reward is contingent upon acceptable behavior by *every* student, peers are reluctant to support undesirable behavior. However, if teachers choose to use group rewards, they should be sure that every student is capable of adhering to the expected standard of behavior. Furthermore, if one or two students fail to respond to group rewards, the strategy should be altered so that all the others are not repeatedly deprived of privileges.

Verbal Reprimands

At some time or another most teachers will use reprimands to manage student behavior, but do reprimands work? Williams (1987) concludes from a review of nine studies that certain forms of verbal reprimands can weaken undesirable behavior in students. For several reasons, however, teachers should be cautious in using reprimands. Reprimands are a form of punishment, and if used repeatedly the student could develop negative reactions toward the teacher and the classroom setting. Teachers should ensure that reprimands are coupled with positive reinforcement for appropriate behavior. No researchers suggest that reprimands be used to substitute for positive interventions. With these cautions in mind, how can reprimands be used constructively?

Recently, Abramowitz, O'Leary, and Futtersak (1988) suggested that short reprimands result in less off-task behavior than long reprimands that encourage "talking back." Earlier research by O'Leary and Becker (1968) and O'Leary, Kaufman, Kass, and Drabman (1970) has also shown that soft reprimands, audible only to the misbehaving student, are more effective than loud reprimands in reducing disruptive classroom behavior. O'Leary et al. (1970) further note the advantages of soft reprimands. First, they do not call the attention of the entire class to the misbehaving student. You will recall from earlier discussions that too much attention to inappropriate behavior could serve as reinforcement for that behavior. Second, because soft reprimands may be different from what disruptive youngsters customarily receive at home or at school, they should be less likely to trigger emotional reactions.

Instructive or Destructive?

Marc surprised Mr. Turner when he retorted, "Go ahead and take me to the principal's office. See if I care!" Mr. Turner didn't really want to take Marc to the office. He realized immediately that he had elicited Marc's stormy reaction by reprimanding Marc loudly in front of his classmates. He knew that threatening Marc was unnecessary, but what could he do now? He didn't want to lose face.

Mr. Turner resolved to change how he reprimanded students in the future. He wanted his corrections to be more instructive than destructive, and he didn't want to treat students any differently than he expected to be treated by his own supervisors and friends.

Van Houten and Doleys (1983) point out in their review of social reprimands that better control of all the variables involved in the delivery of reprimands is needed before concluding that one level of intensity is better than another. For example, if the teacher stands close to students while giving a reprimand, it may be the proximity of the teacher rather than the loudness or softness of the reprimand that is influencing the student. Before you consider using reprimands as a classroom management procedure, we recommend that you examine Van Houten and Doley's (1983) extensive review of the subject.

Response Cost

Response cost is a form of punishment that removes positive reinforcers rather than applying aversive stimuli. Regardless of how mild it might appear, we again suggest that it be used intelligently and with caution. In a typical response cost program, each student earns tokens (e.g., points) for appropriate behavior and forfeits a designated number of tokens for inappropriate behavior. Whatever tokens remain can later be used to purchase back-up privileges. Essentially, a response cost program provides feedback (via tokens earned and forfeited) that appropriate behavior pays but inappropriate behavior costs something.

Walker (1983), who has designed response cost programs and used them extensively, provides a number of recommendations for using response cost effectively. Before implementing a response cost program, he recommends that three preconditions be observed. First, he suggests that the strategy be carefully explained to students. For example, any behavior that will be affected by response cost should be identified and the students informed about the number of points or tokens that can be lost for that behavior. Second, he advises that response cost be tied to a larger reinforcement system that strengthens appropriate behavior. He says that this strategy will make response cost less punitive. And third, he recommends that a response cost delivery-and-feedback system be developed. For example, an effective system would let students know immediately when response cost has been applied, for what, and how many points they have lost. In addition to these preconditions, Walker also provides a number of guidelines for implementing response cost systems in a variety of classroom settings. If you are interested in such a system for your classroom, we suggest that you examine Walker's article as well as another extensive review by Pazulinec, Meyerrose, and Sajwaj (1983).

To Catch a Thief

Should teachers spend time trying to determine who steals? Or, is there a more effective way to reduce stealing? Switzer, Deal, and Bailey (1977) experimented with developing a way to discourage school theft. Their approach involved both group rewards and group response cost. During one phase of this experiment, students in 3 second-grade classes received 10 extra minutes of free time following their snack if nothing had been stolen (reward). If something had been stolen, the teacher left the room to permit return of the item. Return of the stolen item meant students could talk quietly, as usual, during snack, whereas nonreturn of the item meant all students must sit quietly during the snack (response cost). The program proved highly successful. In one class, 37 items had been stolen during an 11 day period when the only control for stealing was a teacher lecture. However, during the reward and response cost phase of the study, only 2 items were stolen and one of those was returned. Similar results were obtained in the other class.

Timeout

Timeout is a brief removal (e.g., five minutes) of a child from a reinforcing setting. As such, the procedure is a form of punishment and should be used with caution. The process is typically used in special education classes and with young students and is applied only to certain forms of misbehavior. Powell and Powell (1982), in a review of the uses and abuses of timeout, suggest that timeout is not equally effective with all disruptive and interfering behavior. They note that timeout works best for managing aggression, temper outbursts, and noncompliant behavior that is maintained by the response of others. They suggest that it is less effective with behavior that is self-stimulating. Rocking and daydreaming would fall into the latter categories. Other excellent reviews of timeout and how to use it are also provided by Brantner and Doherty (1983), Nelson and Rutherford (1983), and Harris (1985).

Because the use of timeout is becoming an increasingly controversial issue, we suggest that you familiarize yourself with alternative forms of discipline and that you talk with other professionals (e.g., the school psychologist or school counselor) before trying to implement any timeout procedure. Parents should also be involved in any decisions regarding the use of timeout. You should also find out if your local school unit has guidelines and policies concerning the use of timeout. Wood and Braaten (1983) make a good case for developing such policies in special education settings, and they offer a number of suggestions, such as having open meetings, for developing guidelines. They also indicate that your state's

Department of Education and its special education unit are good sources of information about policies and guidelines.

Give Me That...

The usefulness of timeout is illustrated in a study by LeBlanc, Busby, and Thomson (1974). The subject of the study was a four-year-old boy who was enrolled in a preschool class with 15 other children. He frequently made physical attacks on other children, called them names, and made demands to "Give me that" or "Shut up." Before trying timeout, the teachers repeatedly tried controlling the child by admonishing him for his aggression. This proved ineffective.

Two types of timeout were then implemented. The first step was removing the youngster from the play area when he misbehaved and placing him in a "timeout chair." If he refused to go to the chair or left before a minute was up without first obtaining permission, he was sent to a timeout room. The timeout strategies were used first in dealing with the physical attacks, then with the name calling, and finally with the inappropriate demands on other children. Each time the timeout strategies were used with his aggressive behavior, the behavior declined immediately to near zero. Soon, only the timeout chair was needed, and eventually that was no longer required.

Natural and Logical Consequences

Instead of resorting to verbal reprimands, response cost, or timeout, some teachers prefer to use what Rudolf Dreikurs (Dreikurs, Brunwald, & Pepper, 1971) calls "natural and logical consequences." Dreikurs argues that most punitive strategies do not emphasize the real consequences of misbehavior. He contends that punishment is something artificially imposed on students, and unlike punishment, natural and logical consequences flow directly from misbehavior. More specifically, a "natural consequence" is an outcome that results from behavior without any artificial arrangement by anyone. For example, a student who is late to class would naturally miss the explanations given at the beginning of the class just as the child who is late for dinner would receive a cold meal. Natural consequences cannot always be used, however. A child who runs into the street would never be allowed to continue the practice because the natural outcome could be fatal.

When natural consequences are inappropriate for the situation, the teacher can use logical ones. Logical consequences are similar to natural ones in that they are directly associated with misconduct, but logical consequences are arranged by the teacher (preferably with the agreement of the misbehaving student). The student who makes a mess, for example, may agree that a logical consequence for this action is to clean up the mess. Similarly, a logical consequence for marking in a book would be to pay damage fees. Although logical consequences are arranged and flow from behavior, Dreikurs (Dreikurs, Brunwald, & Pepper, 1971) contends that students are unlikely to view this approach as punishment when they agree to the terms of the consequences. Incidentally, paddlings and the like are never logical consequences for misbehavior because there is no way in which a paddling is related to or flows logically from a behavior.

Who Is Likely to Use Physical Punishment

We have said nothing about paddlings and other forms of corporal punishment because so many other appropriate strategies are available for managing student behavior. You should know that the use of physical punishment may cause your colleagues to view you in a negative light and can leave you open to other professional dilemmas.

Rust and Kinnard (1983) have suggested that teachers who use corporal punishment tend to be more closed-minded and impulsive than those who do not. They drew this conclusion from a study of 114 teachers from 10 schools in a medium-sized school system in Tennessee. Rust and Kinnard also found that teachers who used heavy punishment had fewer years of teaching experience and a limited array of disciplinary techniques. These teachers were also more likely to have been punished physically themselves while in school. Although these characteristics don't fit everyone who has ever resorted to corporal punishment, users of corporal punishment can expect to receive closer scrutiny in the future as increased efforts are made to improve our schools. Eight states now ban corporal punishment.

About School Violence

No form of excessive student behavior is more on the general public's mind today than episodes of school violence. These include assaults, robbery, and destruction of school property. Can ideas in this and other texts help reduce school violence? Possibly. No text has all the answers, but teachers can defuse many explosive situations merely by increasing their managerial skills. Most youngsters who end up in corrective institutions are products of the public school systems. And while in school, many have exhibited lesser forms of misconduct *before* they got into serious trouble. All acts of violence at school are not a function of teacher ineptness, however. Improvements in family life, affirmative programs by police and the courts, and increased funding for youth-oriented recreation and rehabilitation programs could help alleviate many school-related crimes.

Although teachers are not solely responsible for what occurs in school, they can prevent many violent acts and often keep misbehavior that does occur within manageable dimensions. For example, one teacher in a large junior-high school stopped a fight, settled down cheering onlookers, and limited the problem before it could spread. He accomplished this by working his way through the crowd and telling students he knew (and expected would obey him) to go about their business. The crowd slowly grew smaller as he reached the combatants. He persuaded the two students involved in the fight to sit down and discuss their problem. Unfortunately, this story does not have a good ending. Later in the day the principal learned about the incident and decided on an additional course of action. He found everyone who had been in the crowd (to get all of the details of the fight) and gave them a lecture on the dangers of aggression. He became emotional and so did the students. What earlier had been reduced to a minor incident quickly escalated into a school riot. We are not saying that students should never discuss the hazards of aggression — they should, — but discussions are best conducted in small groups under controlled conditions. Typically, when a fight occurs, only the people directly involved should discuss the incident. Problems should be isolated — not expanded.

Many other skills besides isolating problems can be used to avert violent acts. The strategies for managing behavior that we discussed earlier in the chapter can help lower the incidence of school violence. For example, among the findings of the National Institute of Education (1978) was evidence that violence is lower in schools where students:

- Rate the classroom as well-disciplined, where rules are strictly enforced, and where the principal is considered strict.
- Consider school discipline as being fairly administered.

- Say that classes teach them what they want to know.
- Believe they can influence what happens in their lives by their efforts, rather than feeling that things happen to them which they cannot control.

All of these characteristics are variables that can be directly manipulated by school personnel. Teachers and principals can initiate actions to solve problems. They can be firm without being authoritarian. They can participate in plans to improve home relationships. Teachers can cooperate with police to improve school security. Teachers can also become active in professional organizations aimed at better informing the public of school problems and school needs. Furthermore, teachers can enroll in courses that prepare them for managing school disruptiveness and coping with job-related stress. The list could go on. We believe that teachers should be solution oriented.

Finally, we are not suggesting that teachers and other school personnel will never reach the "end of their ropes" in working with some troubled students. Many schools have tried everything from positive reinforcement to in-school suspension only to discover that an occasional student is unresponsive to all that is tried. In some cases, school personnel conclude that the interests of everyone (including the chronic offenders) are best served by removing these students from school and placing them in the hands of other agencies. There will be failures. Nonetheless, teachers can influence big problems by the way they respond to commonplace disruptions.

Making Choices

Before trying any of the intervention strategies that are described in this chapter, you should consider a number of factors. First, how do you feel about a given intervention strategy? Is there any strategy that you would not want to be subject to? Certainly, you should never use a strategy that you feel is unacceptable.

If you are like most teachers, you will prefer positive strategies for your students. Researchers (Elliott, Witt, Galvin, & Peterson, 1984; Witt, Martens, & Elliott, 1984) have found that teachers rate positive strategies, such as reinforcing behavior incompatible with misconduct, more acceptable for managing problems than negative reinforcement strategies such as timeout. The work of these researchers also suggests that teachers generally prefer easier and less time-consuming strategies over more complex strategies unless the problem being confronted is severe.

With most problems you should consider the opinions and preferences of your students. Turco and Elliott's (1986) research involving fifth, seventh, and ninth graders in two schools indicated that those students were able to differentiate between various methods for improving student behavior. In rating solutions to disruptive behavior, the students showed a strong preference for being disciplined at home for school offenses over public reprimands at school. These researchers noted that the students' preferences for home-based discipline might be explained in two ways. First, the students apparently preferred to pay the consequences for misbehavior in as private a situation as possible: the home happened to be the most private option presented. Second, students might perceive their homes as a place where discipline is lax, or they might view it as a place where more reinforcers are available than is the case at school.

In considering different disciplinary options, the opinions of parents, the school counselor, and the school psychologist should also be considered. Most school systems have guidelines regarding the types of intervention strategies that they consider acceptable for classroom use. Many states also provide special in-service education for teachers that includes training in the use of various disciplinary strategies. When problems are serious enough to merit intervention, they are also serious enough to merit consultation and use of available resources. Consulting others can keep problems from escalating and serve as a means for learning more details about suitable intervention strategies.

Other factors will also guide you in the use of corrective strategies. For example, knowing your students' personalities is important. Some students are very sensitive and need only be reminded of what they should not be doing. To use harsh punishment with such a student would be inadvisable. Similarly, punishment is generally not a viable option until positive strategies have been tried and given a chance to work.

Summary

Teachers are sometimes perplexed about how they should immediately deal with disruptive behavior. Fortunately, a wide range of options are available that have been systematically tested in actual classroom settings so the teacher does not have to rely solely on personal judgement. This chapter has introduced you to a few of those options. These included:

informative feedback; ignoring minor infractions; verbal reprimands; response cost; timeout; several schedules of differential reinforcement; and natural and logical consequences. We also looked briefly at the problem of school violence and suggested that many "big" problems might be averted by the way smaller problems are handled. Suggestions were also given for choosing strategies.

Although you may never have a need to use every strategy that has been mentioned, knowing a range of strategies gives you a better basis for whatever choices you do make. Finally, you should note that frequent occurrences of misconduct may be an indication that changes need to be made in your management strategy. Perhaps the instructional program needs revision, or you may need to examine whether students are being sufficiently reinforced for desired behavior. No strategy should become a substitute for strengthening desirable behavior.

References

Aaron, B. A., & Bostow, D. E. (1978). Indirect facilitation of on-task behavior produced by contingent free-time academic productivity. *Journal of Applied Behavior Analysis, 11*(1), 197.

Abramowitz, A. J., O'Leary, S. G., & Futtersak, M. W. (1988). The relative impact of long and short reprimands on children's off-task behavior in the classroom. *Behavior Therapy, 18,* 243–247.

Ayllon, T., & Roberts, M. D. (1974). Eliminating discipline problems by strengthening academic performances. *Journal of Applied Behavior Analysis, 7,* 71–76.

Brantner, J. P., & Doherty, M. A. (1983). A review of timeout: A conceptual and methodological analysis. In S. Axelrod & J. Apsche (Eds.), *The effects of punishment on human behavior*. New York: Academic Press.

Craig, R. C., Mehrens, W. H., & Clarizio, H. F. (1975). *Contemporary educational psychology*. New York: John Wiley and Sons.

Drabman, R. S., & Lahey, B. B. (1977). Feedback in classroom behavior modification: Effects on the target and her classmates. In K. D. O'Leary & S. G. O'Leary (Eds.), *Classroom management: The successful use of behavior modification* (2nd ed.). New York: Pergamon Press.

Dreikurs, R., Brunwald, B. B., & Pepper, F. C. (1971). *Maintaining sanity in the classroom: Illustrated teaching techniques*. New York: Harper and Row.

Elliott, S. N., Witt, J. C., Galvin, G. A., & Peterson, R. (1984). Acceptability of positive and reductive behavioral interventions: Factors that influence teachers' decisions. *Journal of School Psychology, 22,* 353–360.

Harris, K. R. (1985). Definitional, parametric, and procedural considerations in timeout interventions and research. *Exceptional Children, 51*(4), 279–288.

Kazdin, A. E. (1984). *Behavior modification in applied settings* (3rd ed.). Homewood, IL: Dorsey Press.

Kelly, M. B., & Bushell, D., Jr. (1987). Student achievement and differential reinforcement of incompatible behavior: Hand raising. *Psychology in the Schools, 24,* 273–280.

Kindall, L. M., Workman, E. A., & Williams, R. L. (1980). The consultative merits of praise-ignore versus praise-reprimand instruction. *Journal of School Psychology, 18*(4), 373–380.

LeBlanc, J. M., Busby, H. H., & Thomson, C. L. (1974). The functions of timeout for changing the aggressive behaviors of a preschool child; a multiple-baseline analysis. In R. Ulrich, T. Stachnik, & J. Mabry (Eds.), *Control of human behavior: Behavior modification in education.* Glenview, IL: Scott, Foresman & Co.

Lobitz, W. C., & Burns, W. J. (1977). The "least intrusive intervention" strategy for behavior change procedures: The use of public and private feedback in school classrooms. *Psychology in the Schools, 14*(1), 89–94.

Long, J. D., & Williams, R. L. (1973). The comparative effectiveness of group and individually contingent free time with inner-city junior-high-school students. *Journal of Applied Behavior Analysis, 6,* 465–474.

Madsen, C. H., Jr., Becker, W. C., Thomas, D. R., Koser, L., & Plager, E. (1968). An analysis of the reinforcing function of "sit down" commands. In R. K. Parker (Ed.), *Readings in educational psychology.* Boston: Allyn and Bacon.

Madsen, C. H., Jr., Becker, W. C., & Thomas, D. R. (1968). Rules, praise, and ignoring: Elements of elementary classroom control. *Journal of Applied Behavior Analysis, 1,* 139–150.

The National Institute of Education. (1978). *Violent schools-safe schools: The safe school study report to Congress* (Volume 1). Washington, DC: U.S. Department of Health, Education, and Welfare.

Nelson, C. M., & Rutherford, R. B. (1983). Timeout revisited: Guidelines for its use in special education. *Exceptional Education Quarterly, 3*(4), 56–67.

O'Leary, K. D., & Becker, W. C. (1968). The effects of the intensity of a teacher's reprimands on children's behavior. *Journal of School Psychology, 7,* 8–11.

O'Leary, K. D., Kaufman, K. F., Kass, R., & Drabman, R. (1970). The effects of loud and soft reprimands on the behavior of disruptive students. *Exceptional Children, 37,* 145–155.

O'Leary, K. D., & O'Leary, S. G. (1977). *Classroom management: The successful use of behavior modification* (2nd Ed.). New York: Pergamon Press.

Pazulinec, R., Meyerrose, M., & Sajwaj, T. (1983). Punishment via response cost. In S. Axelrod & J. Apsche (Eds.), *The effects of punishment on human behavior*. New York: Academic Press.

Poling, A., & Ryan, C. (1982). Differential reinforcement-of-other-behavior schedules: Therapeutic applications. *Behavior Modification, 6*(1), 3–21.

Powell, T. H., & Powell, I. Q. (1982). The use and abuse of using timeout procedure for disruptive pupils. *Pointer, 26*(2), 18–22.

Rust, J. O., & Kinnard, K. Q. (1983). Personality characteristics of the users of corporal punishment in the schools. *Journal of School Psychology, 21,* 91–105.

Simon, S., Ayllon, T., & Milan, M. A. (1982). Behavioral compensation: Contrastlike effects in the classroom. *Behavior Modification, 6*(3), 407–420.

Skiba, R. J., Casey, A., & Center, B. A. (1985). Nonaversive procedures in the treatment of classroom behavior problems. *Journal of Special Education, 19* (4), 459–481.

Switzer, E. B., Deal, T. E., & Bailey, J. S. (1977). The reduction of stealing in second graders using a group contingency. *Journal of Applied Behavior Analysis, 10,* 267–272.

Turco, T. L., & Elliott, S. N. (1986). Assessment of students' acceptability ratings of teacher-initiated interventions for classroom misbehavior. *Journal of School Psychology, 24,* 277–283.

Van Houten, R., & Doleys, D. M. (1983). Are social reprimands effective? In S. Axelrod & J. Apsche (Eds.), *The effects of punishment on human behavior*. New York: Academic Press.

Walker, H. M. (1983). Applications of response cost in school settings: Outcomes, issues and recommendations. *Exceptional Education Quarterly, 3*(4), 47–55.

Williams, R. L. (1987). Classroom management. In J. A. Glover & R. R. Ronning (Eds.). *Historical foundations of educational psychology*. New York: Plenum.

Williams, R. L., & Long, J. D. (1983). *Toward a self-managed life style* (3rd ed.). Boston: Houghton Mifflin.

Witt, J. C., Martens, B. K., & Elliott, S. N. (1984). Factors affecting teachers' judgments of the acceptability of behavioral interventions: Time involvement, behavior problem severity, and type of intervention. *Behavior Therapy, 15,* 204–209.

Wood, F. H., & Braaten, S. (1983). Developing guidelines for the use of punishing intervention in the schools. *Exceptional Education Quarterly, 3*(4), 68–74.

CHAPTER 6

The Home Connection: Working with Parents

"Mary, I dread this afternoon. Parent-teacher conferences really make me nervous."

"Yes, I know what you mean. I also get the feeling that some of the parents are uncomfortable."

"I suppose that if I took more time to understand parents' feelings and needs I would be more prepared."

"Yes, I think you would find that you have much to offer parents as well as students."

Have you sometimes felt anxious about impending conferences with parents of your students? If so, you are not alone. Poor parent-teacher communication can undermine even a teacher's best efforts in both instruction and discipline. In this chapter, we will examine ways of understanding, communicating with and involving parents to help develop and maintain a high level of cooperation between the home and the school.

Understanding Parents

Parents' motivation for behaving in certain ways may not be immediately apparent. Perhaps you wondered why Mr. Brown failed to respond to your request for a conference about his son's behavior in the classroom. Or maybe Mrs. Stechini's lack of concern about her child's truancy was puzzling. Why do some parents seem so uninterested in their child's school activities while other parents seem overly concerned? What makes parents tick?

Abraham Maslow (1943), a psychologist who developed a theory of human motivation, provides some insights that may be helpful in explaining parent behavior. To apply Maslow's theory you must first have some background information about the parents and the home environment of your students. For example, you may find that Johnny's mother works the night shift in a garment factory and that he and his siblings are left alone when she is not at home; or Rosa's mother may be active on the fund-raising committee of a local college. Acquiring basic background information about your students will require effort, but the reward can be a better understanding of the students and their parents.

Maslow's Theory

Maslow (1943) says that the key to human development is the gratification of basic needs. Maslow has arranged these basic needs in a sequence or hierarchy from the lowest to the highest, and claims that these constitute the motives for human behavior. Once lower-level needs are met, higher-level needs motivate behavior.

Maslow's (1943) hierarchy of needs includes physiological needs such as food, water, and relief from discomfort or pain; safety needs such as an environment that offers a sense of security or a secure job or income; social needs such as the need for acceptance by others and the hunger for affection; and esteem needs such as the desire for recognition and prestige and the desire to have one's accomplishments respected.

Once basic needs are met, a person is freed for self-actualization, a state of being that results from the commitment of talents to causes outside the cause of self. The self actualized person has realized his or her potential. Few people are truly self-actualized although many individuals may be well into the process of self-actualization. Self-actualization is also very difficult to maintain because lower-level needs may repeatedly become predominant and require attention.

Once a need is met, it no longer functions as a motivator unless the situtation changes to threaten or prevent the continued attainment of the need. For example, losing a job has an impact on both security and self-esteem for most individuals. Initially, the person who loses the job may be concerned about the higher-level need, that is, esteem, and may be embarrassed to tell friends. However, as savings dwindle, esteem needs usually become secondary to more basic security needs and friends may be approached for help in finding work. Once the new job is secure, the esteem needs reemerge. It is possible to be motivated by needs at more than one level, but one need will often be paramount.

Maslow's (1943) hierarchy can be depicted as follows:

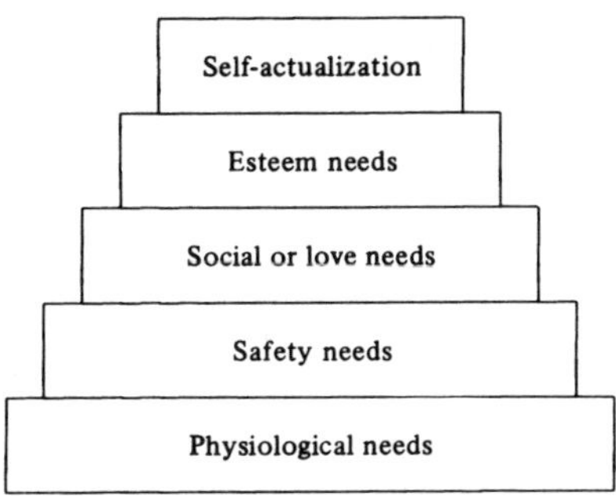

Application of Maslow's Theory

Let's look at ways of applying Maslow's theory to the understanding of parents. Consider an example that may occur in your work. Hector is a well-dressed, socially outgoing second-grade boy from an upper-middle-class home. Both of his parents are well-known and respected professionals. Although Hector seems to have average ability, he is experiencing a great deal of trouble in all academic areas. You suspect a learning disability or perhaps a more global learning problem. School records indicate that his achievement was below average in first grade and that he was passed to the second grade with reservations. His parents respond to your request for a parent-teacher conference and are amenable to your suggestion that psychological testing be scheduled.

When the test results indicate Hector's ability is on the low side of average, more within the slow-learner range, and when resource help is recommended, the parents categorically reject the assessment results as well as the recommendation. They insist that Hector's problems indict the teacher and the school for not doing their jobs. Both strongly protest that there is no history of learning problems in their respective extended families and state that they refuse to have Hector labeled "slow" by sending him to the resource room. Is the parents' reaction surprising? Not in light of Maslow's hierarchy of needs. Very likely, they have met their physical, safety, and social needs while esteem needs are continuing to motivate their behavior. Being told that their son is slow no doubt represents a blow to their self-esteem as well as to their self-perceived position in the community. Their lack of cooperation may involve an attempt to continue to meet their esteem needs by denying that their son has a problem. If the teacher or the school can be found culpable, the threat to their self-esteem is removed.

Consider another example. June is an unkempt eight-year-old child who is frequently absent. She does poorly on all her schoolwork. Your repeated notes to her parents have not been answered. Following some detective work on your part, you find that June and her four siblings live with their mother in a very dilapidated apartment several blocks from school. They have recently been evicted from a better apartment due to nonpayment of rent, not the first time that this has occurred within the last two years. Mrs. Clancy, June's mother, is hardworking but earns minimal wages. One of June's siblings has a chronic illness.

What does Maslow's theory contribute to your understanding of Mrs. Clancy? First, this mother is struggling to meet the very basic needs of food and shelter (physiological and safety needs.) Second, her daughter's poor school records do not threaten her self-esteem because her energies are being expended to meet lower-level needs. In effect, her unstated but overt stance is basically: "I can't worry about that right now when I may not have enough money to pay this month's bills." Until Mrs. Clancy is able to adequately meet the basic needs of her family, it is unlikely that higher-level needs will function as significant motivators for her behavior.

Do Parents' Needs Matter?

Is parental training involvement alone enough to overcome the behavior problems of children from underprivileged homes? Dumas and Albin (1986) found that it is not. In a study of 82 families with aggressive, noncompliant children, these researchers found that parents' attendance at parent-training meetings and cooperation with program instructions did not have a significant impact on the behavior of their children. However, social factors such as whether both parents were present in the home, marital violence, psychopathological symptoms in the mother, family income, and educational level of the mother were found to be related to treatment failure. Dumas and Albin speculated that families with economic and social problems may be unable to benefit from parent training regardless of their level of involvement. These families may require supportive services such as personal or financial counseling before they can benefit from parent training programs. In Maslow's (1943) terms, lower-level needs must receive attention before higher-level needs become motivators for behavior.

Maslow's (1943) needs hierarchy can help teachers understand what motivates parents. When parents react unexpectedly, it may be that the needs that are motivating their behavior fall outside the teacher's realm of expectations.

Understanding why parents respond as they do is one thing. Eliciting their agreement and involvement toward a common goal is another. For example, how can you work with Hector's parents to meet the goal of improving his academic performance? Your task involves helping his parents see that in providing remedial assistance for Hector their own achievement goals for him can be accomplished. In the case of Mrs. Clancy, you may want to help her locate resources such as subsidized housing. With all parents, you will need to agree on common goals, develop strategies for change, and plan for evaluation and redirection as needed.

Parent-Teacher Anxiety

Parents sometimes intimidate teachers. The reverse is also true. Often the mutual anxiety felt by both parties has a detrimental effect on parent-teacher relationships. In addition to considering parents' actions in light of Maslow's (1943) hierarchy of needs, you may also find it helpful to remember that parents were also once students with varying school experiences. Parents entering a classroom may face a flood of memories, both positive and negative. They may have faced ridicule, or failed to complete school. Graduation from school may not be within the realm of their personal experience or that of their family. Their concept of themselves as successful parents may be very low. The teacher may represent an authority figure with whom they do not agree but with whom they feel powerless to disagree. As a result, they may protect themselves by assuming a passive role. That is, they may simply fail to act on any of the suggestions made by the teacher.

Communicating with Parents

Increasing your understanding of parents will not, in itself, create positive home-school relationships. It is also important to communicate with parents at a level that is mutually satisfying for both parties. Essentially, communication should allow for the transfer and understanding of information and/or feelings. It is a complex process that may involve a one-way or a two-way information system. Examples of one-way communication include bulletins or newspapers. Two-way communication, in contrast, involves the participation of all parties, e.g., teacher and parent (Bullock & Reilly, 1981) . People usually think of phoning, conversing, or writing letters when communication is mentioned; however, communication also involves nonverbal actions. For example, we often send messages to others by the tone of our voice, by our body posture, or via eye contact. Sometimes our nonverbal messages conflict with our verbal messages. A teacher in a parent-teacher conference may verbally express interest in a student while displaying nonverbal actions that suggest impatience or failure to listen. In this case, the message received by the parent will most likely be the negative nonverbal message rather than the positive verbal one.

Learn to Listen

What can you do to improve your communication skills? One important step is to improve your listening skills. In order to do this, you may have to make a conscious effort to talk less and allow parents to express their concerns. Talking and listening are mutually exclusive. You must also communicate nonverbally that you are interested in what is being said. For example, you should make eye contact with the speaker and avoid tapping your feet, fidgeting in your chair, or shuffling papers. Do not interrupt. While you may, at times, anticipate what the speaker is going to say, you should allow the speaker the opportunity to say it. Don't be in a hurry. Try to put yourself in the speaker's place. Ask questions and reiterate your understanding of what has been said. You may be surprised at the improvement in your communication with parents if you master the technique of being a good listener.

Have You Heard This?

Have you noticed that certain themes repeatedly appear in parents' questions during parent-teacher conferences? The Instructor *(''Questions,'' 1984) reports that topics such as discipline, reading, and family are frequently mentioned. Examples of questions that are often asked include:*

1. *How do I get my child to cooperate when I ask him/her to do something?*
2. *How do I help my child learn to read?*
3. *How can both parents stay involved in their child's education after a parental divorce?*

4. How can schools be more sensitive to nontraditional families such as stepfamilies and single parents?

5. What can the school system do to help me as a working parent stay involved with my child's education?

Answers for these questions were provided in the Instructor *("Questions," 1984) and teachers were invited to share copies with parents. You may also want to look at this resource before your next parent-teacher conference.*

Ask for Feedback

In addition to listening to parents, you must also be able to convey information to them. You may sometimes feel that they are not listening or do not understand what you have to say. At such times, you may want to have them reiterate to you their understanding of what has been said. This technique should allow you to clear up misunderstandings that might otherwise interfere with your relationship and impair further communication. If you find that parents are distorting what you say or if you detect hostility, anger, or strong defensiveness, communication has probably broken down. In that case, you will need to search for common points of agreement and renew the communication process.

Parent Conferences

Parent-teacher conferences are a frequently used technique for communicating with parents. Bullock and Reilly (1981) offer suggestions for increasing the effectiveness of communication during these meetings. Their ideas include developing preplanned objectives in order to keep the conference on target and to allow for discussion of elements that are deemed important. Parents should be allowed to contribute to the agenda. Going over the topics to be discussed and adding parent concerns should be done at the beginning of the meeting. The teacher should be prepared with documentation if topics such as a child's lack of progress are to be discussed. Some examples of satisfactory work should also be provided regardless of the discussion topics.

Bullock and Reilly (1981) also stress the importance of respect, (i.e., giving parents the opportunity to express their opinions, raise questions, and provide feedback). Encourage parents to ask questions to clarify problems and insure comprehension. Further, be sensitive to the feelings that underlie what is said. Communication should be adjusted to the level of the parents. Teachers should avoid making assumptions, such as that a parent has the skills to help a child with math, and should be sensitive to the beliefs, values, and concerns of minority-group students and parents. Finally, Bullock and Reilly indicate that promptness and brevity are important. However, the meetings should not be so brief as to impede effective two-way communication.

Appreciating Cultural Differences

Ms. Murphey, a sixth-grade teacher, recently relocated to a new city. Her first introduction to her new classroom yielded an array of names that were unfamiliar to her and suggested that a great deal of cultural diversity was present in her classroom. Ms. Murphey decided to take advantage of the differences by devising teaching units that would allow students to share unique aspects of their cultural background with others. She reasoned that such an approach would increase students' knowledge and foster an appreciation of the cultural differences.

In planning for parent-teacher conferences, Ms. Murphey spent time researching cultural differences and strategies for working with families and children from different backgrounds. Her goal was to understand the values, beliefs, and concerns of her students' families. She reviewed her expectations for each student in light of her knowledge about the students' background. During the conferences, she encouraged parents to provide their expectations both of her and their child. Some beliefs were very similar to her own while others were widely divergent. By considering each parent an ally and a resource, Ms. Murphey was able to satisfactorily complete all parent conferences. In the process, she attained a better understanding of each student and an appreciation for the motivations underlying some of her students' behavior.

Rabbitt (1978) outlined the three elements of a successful conference: (a) giving information; (b) getting information; and (c) finding solutions to academic and behavioral problems. When these three elements are used as a basic outline, it bccomes easier for teachers to plan productive conferences. Evaluation is another important facet of the conference that should be completed by the teacher following each conference. Only by evaluating what has been successful or unsuccessful in the past can future conferences be improved.

Tips for teachers. Rathbun (1978) provides several strategies for improving parent-teacher conferences and suggests several traps to avoid. Initially, she suggests that conferences be scheduled at a time when both parent and teacher can talk without interruption. She stresses the importance of putting the parent at ease and offers the following suggestions:

1. Be friendly in greeting the parent.
2. Check the names of the parents immediately before the conference. Susie Cohen's mother may have been divorced and is now Mrs. Aronson. Do not assume that the child's surname is also the parent's surname.
3. Do not assume that an older parent is a grandparent.
4. Give your own name clearly, then refer to the child you intend to discuss. Some parents may have more than one conference scheduled on a particular day.

Other basic strategies suggested by Rathbun (1978) include:

1. Arrange the room so you can sit at a table beside a parent or have the conference in a conference room. Don't sit behind your desk while parents sit in student desks or on folding chairs.
2. Plan for the conference so that you have information about the child at your fingertips.
3. Make a list of the child's grades. Otherwise, parents may wish to look at your grade book.
4. Remain flexible, but have a general plan about what you want to cover at the conference.

Common traps to avoid include:

1. Generalities. Parents respond best when they are provided with specific information (e.g., "It may help increase Gloria's maturity if she is given a weekly list of chores that you see she completes.") Saying "Gloria is immature" provides little help to the parents.
2. Double-talk. Parents appreciate straight talk about the problem their child is having.

3. Amateur psychology. Do not attempt to psychoanalyze when discussing the child.
4. Rudeness. Remain polite even if you feel parents are being antagonistic.

Teachers occasionally feel overwhelmed and perhaps frightened at the idea of conducting individual parent conferences. Parents may feel the same way about meeting and talking with teachers. They may be especially concerned they will be told that their child is not doing as well as they thought or hoped. Thus, both the teacher and parent may be ill at ease at the initial meeting. Beginning the conference on a positive note can help to ease tensions. Showing the parents examples of their child's work that are especially commendable or that demonstrate progress is a good way to begin. Recounting a positive story about their child can also help parents feel positive and thus help reduce your feelings of tension. Academic and behavioral elements that need improvement should be discussed; however, conferences should begin and end on a positive note.

"Mr. Walters sometimes has a little difficult handling parent conferences."

Sometimes, teachers are faced with parents who are dissatisfied either with some past incident or with a school procedure. Parents can occasionally be irate. How does a teacher deal with an angry parent? You should try to dissipate outbursts of emotion in order to reap benefits for the student. To achieve this you must refrain from becoming angry in these situations.

The following suggestions may be helpful in coping with such a crisis:

1. Refuse to conduct the conference in the classroom when students are nearby. Firmly insist on arranging a conference for a later hour.
2. Remain unemotional when conducting the conference. Try not to take comments personally. Remember, the parents are probably concerned and upset over what they perceive is happening to their child, and their perception may or may not be correct. Try to determine how the parents perceive the incident and solicit their views on a solution. These views will often be expressed anyway, but asking for their opinion helps convey your desire to help.
3. Respond to the feelings that lie behind parental statements rather than the content (e.g., "You are really concerned about. . . ." or ". . . makes you very angry"). This communicates to parents that you really understand and reduces the likelihood of direct conflict.
4. Help the parents explore the ramifications of different solutions with the goal of providing for the best interests of the child. Attempt to work out at least a beginning solution to the problem. If possible, arrange for both you and the parents to be responsible for some aspect of implementation.
5. Arrange for continued communication. Ask the parents to call and report, positively or negatively, on what has happened since the conference. Do not be afraid to say, "I don't know"; "I have tried"; "I need your advice"; "This may not work"; "I may be wrong"; or "Call me if things don't go well." Hearing teachers admit that they may not always be right can go a long way in defusing an irate parent.

Therapeutic Parent Conferences

While most parent-teacher conferences primarily involve exchange of information, a model for moving beyond the superficiality of the typical conference to therapeutic intervention has been proposed.

Simon (1984) makes the point that families with the most need for services are often most resistant to accepting therapy referrals. He suggests that parent conferences be designed to be therapeutic as well as informative.

Simon (1984) offers four goals when discussing a child's behavior problems at parent conferences: (a) to ultimately change the behavior of the child in a positive direction; (b) to shift the responsibility for directing the focus for change to the parents; (c) to make the school problem an issue for the home; and (d) to reach a mutual agreement as to the concrete steps to be taken to deal with the problem.

Simon (1984) proposes that the school professional, usually a counselor, be in charge of the conference and that both the parent (or parents) and the student be involved. A circular seating arrangement is suggested. The school professional is responsible for moving the conference forward so that the established goals are accomplished. He describes the four stages of a successful therapeutic conference as follows:

1. *Orientation: Activities during this stage include describing the problem and emphasizing that the goal of the conference is to change behavior and develop an action plan.*
2. *Discussion and Negotiation: Simon suggests that during this phase of the conference parents be asked to tell their child directly what changes they want made and that parents be encouraged to take charge in resolving the problem. An action plan should be developed.*
3. *Contract: During this stage of the conference, expected behavior should be delineated clearly in behavioral terms and rewards and punishments should be specified. It is recommended that each person be given an assigned task.*
4. *Summary: The school professional reviews the action of the conference in this final phase.*

Simon (1984) stresses that teachers should help parents assume responsibility for changing their child's behavior. To quote Simon: "Parental involvement in interventions is essential to facilitate significant behavior change on the part of the child or adolescent" (p. 612).

Clearly, a therapeutic orientation is not necessary for most parent-teacher conferences; however, Simon's suggestions could prove useful in situations involving students with behavioral problems whose parents will not follow through on therapy referrals.

Both parents and teachers would like for students to become happy, productive citizens. Parental support and cooperation are important factors in reaching this goal, and most parents are willing to help in whatever way they can to insure that their child gets a good education. Unfortunately, parents are usually consulted only when their child has broken a rule, fails to attend school regularly, or is not keeping pace academically. Few teachers remember that parents would also like to know when their child has performed especially well or has exhibited exemplary behavior. Parents appreciate knowing when their child has had a good day. They like to know that their child is making progress, even though it may be minimal. Parents will be more cooperative with the teacher and the school when they receive positive as well as negative feedback about their child.

All desirable behavior exhibited by students need not be communicated to parents. Few teachers have time to write even monthly notes. However, seeing that each child carries home a note once each grading period commending their progress will foster the positive attitudes of parents and improve teacher-parent relationships.

Parents usually know their children well, their likes and dislikes, and can often tell a teacher what works and does not work with them. They can frequently provide information that is helpful in reducing inappropriate classroom behavior or in increasing desired behavior. Occasionally, students present problems that are more easily resolved by a joint effort rather than by the parents or teacher working alone.

Parent-teacher conferences should be scheduled at least twice each year. Some schools have experimented with providing student holidays during the time parents are scheduled for private conferences with the teacher. Whatever approach you choose, remember to schedule a few conferences in the evenings to accommodate parents who work during the day. Child care and parenting courses should also be offered in the evening (''Questions,'' 1984).

Involving Parents

Research during the last decade shows home and community environments are vitally linked to student success (Mattox & Rich, 1977). Therefore, these influences should be cultivated and directed toward maximal student development. As a beginning, teachers may want to talk with parents about how they view the abilities of their children. Miller (1986) has found that the more accurately mothers are able to gauge their child's cognitive ability, the better the child's performance. From these findings, Miller speculates that mothers are better able to provide an appropriate and challenging learning environment when they can accurately gauge their child's abilities. Teachers should help parents recognize their child's strengths and weaknesses by having honest discussions with them. It is important, however, that information about the child be presented in a positive light and that weaknesses be counterbalanced by discussing strengths.

Parent Involvement and the School

Epstein (1984) surveyed 3,698 teachers and principals concerning their attitudes toward parent involvement and their techniques for getting parents to promote learning at home. From these teachers, 82 were selected and grouped according to the strategies they used for parent involvement. The parents of these teachers' students were also surveyed. Home-learning activities used by the teachers included reading, informal learning, discussion, tutoring, and contracts. Results indicated that teachers who invited parents into their classrooms and to workshops were more likely to request that parents become involved in all five types of home-learning activities. Unfortunately, only a few parents chose to be active at school. Those who received frequent requests to become involved or other kinds of school-home communications reported an increased understanding about school and about how to help their children. These parents were also better able to assess teacher merits.

Consider Parents' Feelings

Involving parents is not easy, and some teachers have become discouraged in their attempts to work with parents. Many parents are busy with their jobs and have little time to devote to the formal education of their child; some parents do not value education highly; some parents feel that they do not have the skills to teach their children; and others believe that it's your job to reach their child and they should not be expected to contribute. As a rule, however, parents have strong feelings of love for their children and the child's welfare is usually their primary concern. They will attempt to cooperate with the teacher or school authorities even though they have misgivings about what they are asked to do. Teachers should take care to insure that the ideas they present to parents are both workable and likely to suceed for that particular child. A method of evaluating success and failure should be given to the parents. Casual suggestions made by teachers may be taken seriously by parents and rigorously implemented. Failure can create anxiety if parents blame themselves for not doing things correctly although the technique itself may prove inappropriate. Parents should be told, "This may be helpful, but if it doesn't work, we will try something else."

Promote Learning at Home

How might you involve the parents of your students in promoting student learning? Fredericks et al. (1983) provide some very basic suggestions that can be copied and given to parents. They include:

1. Encourage your child by praising efforts and accomplishments.
2. Make sure your child gets enough rest (eight to nine hours of sleep).
3. Keep your child healthy by taking him or her to the doctor for regular checkups, providing well-balanced meals, maintaining cleanliness, encouraging regular exercise, and notifying the teacher of any medical problems.
4. See that your child attends school regularly.
5. Set aside a regular study time and place.
6. Monitor television viewing.
7. Keep in touch with teachers.
8. Read to your child and encourage him or her to read.

Of all types of parent involvement, the most educationally significant appears to be supervising learning activities at home (Epstein & Becker, 1982). Teachers can give parents specific tasks to work on with their children. For example, parents can be asked to help students find specific details in a reading passage, paraphrase the passage, or answer questions about a character. Parents need to be given several strategies for teaching and reinforcing skills so they can give ongoing support for their children's educational efforts (Fredericks et al., 1983).

Tips for Parents

The Kentucky Department of Education ("How to help") provides parents with a printed list of suggestions for helping their child in school. Their tips include: (a) help the student develop good work habits by providing a quiet place where the student can work; (b) establish a regular time for study; (c) help the student build gradually toward a longer study period by starting with shorter study times; (d) praise and reward the student for completing agreed-upon work; (e) chart the student's progress; and (f) be consistent. Parents can also set the stage for learning by acting as models during study time, (e.g., by reading or bookkeeping). Parents should also talk to their child about school during nonstudy times and expose their children to educational and cultural events outside of school. Other tips for parents include: make sure your child is keeping up homework requirements by checking with the teacher; have realistic expectations; praise more than punish; and provide success experiences.

Becker and Epstein (1983) surveyed teacher opinions of 14 techniques for promoting parent involvement and concluded that reading is the skill that most teachers would like for parents to stress (parents should both read to the child and listen to the child read). Other techniques proposed by Becker and Epstein were not as popular with teachers but they are strategies that may be extremely helpful under certain circumstances. These include: (a) ask parents to initiate discussions with their child about daily school activities, homework assignments, and specific television programs; (b) send suggestions home for activities related to schoolwork and how to use the home environment to stimulate interest in reading; (c) ask parents to supervise homework and to provide rewards and punishments for school performance; (d) ask parents to observe your class; and (e) assist parents in making supplementary learning materials to use at home. Becker and Epstein reported than 84% of the teachers agreed that parents who spend time at school make a greater effort to help their child learn at home.

Creating an Optimal Home Environment for Young Children

What can parents do to optimize the learning environment for their own children? Bradley (1987) summarized research findings in this area and proposed a number of suggestions related to three broad areas of the child's environment: social; cognitive; and physical. A responsive social environment for young children is said to contain the following elements:

1. *Frequent contact with a small number of adults.*
2. *Family members who are sensitive to infant cues.*
3. *Family members who meet a child's needs in a reasonable time, but who also don't anticipate these needs before they are expressed.*
4. *Warm, nurturing families who provide structure and limits on the child's behavior, communicate behavioral expectations, do not use harsh punishment, and reward desirable behavior.*
5. *Family members who are not overly restrictive, who let the child explore, but who also arrange a safe and varied environment.*

Bradley lists the following factors as conducive to cognitive development:

1. *A home environment where children are exposed to frequent and varied use of language.*
2. *Family members who help the child label objects and events and who provide symbolic solutions to problems.*
3. *An environment that provides wide and varied sensory and social experiences.*
4. *Family members who are involved with the child for long periods, who teach the child new concepts and skills, help the child understand personal experiences, and who reinforce the child's own attempts at mastery of the environment.*

Bradley (1987) suggests that the physical environment be structured to provide:

1. *A variety of accessible play materials which the child can comprehend and manipulate.*
2. *Active involvement of family members in playful and instructional activities with the child.*
3. *A regular schedule.*
4. *A reasonably well-lit home, free of household clutter and high levels of background noise.*

Summary

This chapter provided suggestions for developing good relationships between home and school. The importance of understanding parents' needs was also stressed. Communication techniques were discussed and tips for conducting successful parent-teacher conferences were provided. Attention was also given to involving parents in educational endeavors of their child. The parent-teacher conference checklist at the end of this chapter provides a summary of guidelines for your use.

One does not relate successfully to parents, or to any individual, as a result of having read a book. The ideas presented in this chapter should be helpful in increasing positive parent-teacher involvement, but you should be familiar with the techniques for increasing positive interpersonal interaction. You must recognize the feelings and work of others. Parents can provide many insights with regard to their child, for they know the child better than anyone. They are valuable resources. We suggest that you make a commitment to a strong parent-involvement program.

PARENT-TEACHER CONFERENCE CHECKLIST:

Did You Remember to:	Yes	No	Results and Recommendations
A. Plan ahead 1. Give the parents options for conference times.			
2. Send home reminder notes of time and date of conference.			
3. Put your name, grade and room number outside door.			
4. Provide comfortable seating and reading materials for parents who are waiting for conferences.			
5. Put a note on the door, "I am in conference. Please be seated," in order that the parent will not have to peek in the room to see if a conference is in progress.			
6. Arrange the conference room to allow comfortable seating.			
7. Place your chair so you will not be behind a desk.			
8. Put pertinent information on the child in a convenient file or folder.			

Did You Remember to:	Yes	No	Results and Recommendations
9. Have a folder of the child's work.			
10. Make a list of the child's grades.			
11. Develop preplanned objectives.			
12. Check the name of the parent before the conference.			
13. Consider wearing a name tag.			
B. Consider parents' feelings 1. Be friendly.			
2. Be flexible — allow the parent to contribute to the agenda.			
3. Avoid rudeness — whatever the provocation.			
4. Avoid attempting to be a psychiatrist.			
C. Follow a basic agenda 1. Give your own name clearly and refer to the name of the child.			
2. Begin the conference on a positive note by: a. Recounting a positive behavioral incident about the child or b. Show an example of good work by the child			
3. Develop goals and objectives.			
4. Avoid speaking in generalities and double-talk.			
5. Let the parent know how follow-up will be handled.			
6. Thank the parent for coming.			
D. Evaluate 1. Did the parents seem at ease?			
2. Were you able to accomplish your objective for the meeting?			
3. Were goals developed during the conference?			

References

Becker, H. J., & Epstein, J. L. (1983). Teacher practices and parent involvement. *The Education Digest, 83,* 46–49.

Bradley, R. H. (1987). Providing a stimulating and supportive home environment for young children. *Early Childhood Update, 3,* 1, 4.

Bullock, L., & Reilly, T. F. (1981). Talking it over: How parents and school professionals can work together. *Education Unlimited, 3,* 49–50.

Dumas, J. E., & Albin, J. B. (1986). Parent training outcome: Does active parental involvement matter? *Behavior Research and Therapy, 24,* 227–230.

Epstein, J. L. (1984). School policy and parent involvement: Research results. *Educational Horizons, 62,* 70–72.

Epstein, J. L., & Becker, H. J. (1982). Teachers' reported practices of parent involvement: Problems and possibilities. *The Elementary School Journal, 83,* 103–113.

Fredericks, A., Harrington, A., Hill, B., Hunter, M., Loesch, P., Pasztor, J., & Simms, S. (1983). How to talk to parents and get the message home. *Instructor, 93,* 64–66.

How to help your child in school. Publication number 8000000–181. Kentucky Department of Education [1986?].

Maslow, A. H. (1943). A theory of human motivation. *Psychological Review, 50,* 370–396.

Mattox, B., & Rich, D. (1977). Community involvement activities: Research into action. *Theory into Practice, 16,* 29–34.

Miller, S. A. (1986). Parents' beliefs about their children's cognitive abilities. *Developmental Psychology, 22,* 276–284.

Questions parents ask! (1984). *Instructor, 94,* 72–78.

Rabbitt, J. (1978). The parent/teacher conference: Trauma or teamwork? *Phi Delta Kappan, 49,* 471–472.

Rathbun, D. (1978). Parent-teacher talks: Conferences or confrontation? *Learning, 7,* 54–55.

Simon, D. J. (1984). Parent conferences as therapeutic moments. *The Personnel and Guidance Journal, 62,* 612–615.

CHAPTER 7

They Have a Right: Meeting the Needs of Exceptional Students

"I was so worried about how I would handle the handicapped children who have been integrated into my classroom, but mainstreaming them seems to have worked out very well."

"I think careful planning is the key to successful integration. You have certainly made a good effort to make sure that things go smoothly."

Major changes in dealing with handicapped children have occurred since the Education for All Handicapped Children Law, PL 94–142, was passed in 1975. In this chapter, we will delineate the main provisions of this law, describe the different types of exceptionality that it covers, list ways to recognize referral cases, and propose some general techniques for successfully integrating these children into the regular classroom.

Education for the Handicapped

School systems throughout the United States have expanded their services for special-needs students as a result of PL 94–142. Exceptional children ranging from the severely multihandicapped to the intellectually gifted are now able to enjoy educational benefits that were often unavailable to them in the past. The right of the handicapped to a free public education has been ensured and procedures for implementing the educational process have been clearly specified. The law has had a far-reaching impact on the educational systems of our nation.

Appropriate Free Public Education

PL 94–142 stipulates that all children shall be guaranteed a free and appropriate public education. Under the law, all handicapped children between the ages of 3 and 18 were entitled to educational services as of September 1, 1978, and all handicapped individuals between the ages of 3 and 21 were entitled to these services by September 1, 1980. Legislation was later enacted (Education of the Handicapped Amendments 1986) to expand services under the Education for All Handicapped Children Act to: (a) service children ages 3–5 through a mandated preschool program; (b) establish an Early Intervention State Grant Program for infants and toddlers (to age 2); and (c) improve or expand some discretionary programs within the Education of the Handicapped Act (PL 99–457). Basically, PL 99–457 provides that all handicapped children between the ages of 3 and 5 must be served by the 1991–92 school year. States are also eligible to apply for funds to develop early intervention programs to serve the infant through 2-year age group. Under the law, children receiving preschool services will be accorded the basic rights and protection as defined under PL 94–142. The timetable and procedures for implementing the law may vary and it is therefore very important to keep abreast of the services provided in your state.

Individual Education Plan

PL 94–142 requires that an individualized educational plan (IEP) be developed for each child who receives special education services. The IEP must be written to include the level of functioning of the child, long- and short-term goals, services to be provided, criteria for evaluation, extent to which the child will be involved in regular classes and special-education classes, initiation date, and proposed duration of the services. The IEP is to be developed at a planning conference that includes the parent, child (when appropriate), teacher, someone who has recently evaluated the child, and others at the discretion of the parent. IEP meetings must be held annually.

Least-restrictive Environment

PL 94–142 provides the handicapped child with the right to be educated in the least-restrictive environment. This requirement means that, insofar as possible, the child should be educated in the "mainstream" of the school. Some children's individual educational plans will require alternate placements, such as self-contained special-education classes, but in these cases an agency is required to insure that the handicapped child has the opportunity to participate with nonhandicapped children in other school activities.

Access to Records

Parents of handicapped children must be allowed complete access to the educational records of their child by the agency providing the educational service. Included is the right to see all evaluations that determine the child's placement. Parents also have the right to present evidence to amend a child's record. When these cases are ruled against the parents, they have the right to insert into the record a written statement expressing their objection.

Due Process

The intent of PL 94–142 is to insure that decisions concerning the educational placement of the handicapped child be made in his or her best interests. To this end, parents are given the right to participate in the evaluative and decision-making process. When parents and an agency are unable to agree, either party has the right to request an impartial hearing to resolve the disagreement.

Exceptional Children

Most of the children who require special education services fall into nine basic categories: mental retardation; learning disabled; speech/language impaired; hearing impaired; physical/health impaired; emotionally disturbed; multihandicapped; autistic; and gifted.

Mental Retardation

The American Association on Mental Deficiency defines mental retardation as "significantly subaverage intellectual functioning existing concurrently with deficits in adaptive behavior and manifested during the developmental period" (Grossman, 1983). Severity of mental retardation can range from mild to profound. Regular classroom teachers are most likely to have contact only with students who are mildly retarded. These students have an impaired ability to think abstractly and to understand complex verbal explanations. It is frequently necessary to use concrete or tangible reinforcers in working with them. They also have a short memory span. Rewards and punishments should immediately follow their

"Hi! I'm Ed Wilkins from Title II, and this is Bob Cushing from Title IV and Bill Stuart from Title VII. What's your title?"

behavior or they may not be able to make the connection between the behavior and its consequence. They are often easily distracted and respond best when extraneous stimuli are eliminated and cues are emphasized. Mentally retarded children do not generalize well from one situation to another. In order to help increase the probability that they will use a learned behavior in a new and appropriate setting, a variety of situations and experiences should be used in teaching the new behavior. Despite these limitations, do not forget that mentally retarded children experience the same range of emotions (e.g., hurt, anger, and frustration) as your other students do. Make sure their educational program provides them with frequent success experiences.

Learning Disabled

A learning disabled child has traditionally been described as "a child who has a disorder in one or more of the basic learning processes which may manifest itself in significant difficulties in the acquisition and use of listening, speaking, reading, writing, spelling, or performing mathematical calculations" (Tennessee Department of Education, 1982). A new definition proposed by Brown and Campione (1986) shifts the focus from the underlying mental deficit to the skills that the student does possess. For example, a learning-disabled child might exhibit a knowledge deficit such as inadequate decoding skills as opposed to a memory deficit such as poor auditory memory. This domain-specific approach carries important implications for remediation. Once the knowledge deficit is identified, instruction can be targeted to teach the necessary skills.

In order for a child with a suspected learning disability to qualify for special services, many school systems require that you document a significant discrepancy between achievement levels and intellectual functioning. Children who show this discrepancy but are also mentally retarded, environmentally disadvantaged, or emotionally disturbed are typically not included under the classification of "learning disabled." Most learning disabled children are served in the regular classroom and receive supplementary resource assistance in the area of their disability. These children frequently experience frustration in meeting academic demands and may sometimes misbehave when they are unable to cope with classroom stresses. Their activity level is often high and some may have short attention spans. Their self-concepts may also be poor due to repeated failure. Breaking their work down to smaller units, providing for frequent success experiences, and experimenting with alternative teaching techniques can help these students profit from regular classroom instruction. Identifying specific knowledge deficits can also provide invaluable information for corrective action.

Speech/Language Impaired

Speech-impaired children exhibit problems articulating speech sounds. These problems are sometimes identified by parents, physicians, or preschool teachers during the child's early years; however, they often go unnoticed until the child reaches first grade. Some speech/language-impaired children exhibit problems with fluency (e.g., they may stutter), while others may have an abnormal voice quality. Language impairments may involve both receptive understanding and expressive ability. Speech/language-impaired children are usually placed in regular classrooms and receive speech and/or language therapy on a supplementary basis. Therefore, the regular teacher should be aware of the needs of these children and give them ample time to communicate when they are having problems. Attention should not be called to their speech disorder.

Visually Impaired

Visually handicapped children may be totally blind or they may have limited or partial vision. The term ''legal blindness'' is used to describe individauls who have visual acuity of 20/200 or less in the better eye after correction and who have a restricted field of 20 degrees or less (Tennessee Department of Education, 1982). Completely blind children require Braille and nonvisual tactile or auditory materials. Visually limited students may be able to use printed materials, though adaptations such as large print materials will probably be necessary. Many visually impaired students are now served in regular classrooms. The regular classroom teacher, through consultation with a resource specialist for the visually handicapped, can be very successful in meeting their needs.

Hearing Impaired

Hearing impairment can range from total deafness to a mild hearing loss. Some hearing-impaired children learn best through manual communication (for example, sign language) while others may be able to use verbal-communication modalities with some adaptations. The student may wear a hearing aid, for example. Many hearing-impaired students are integrated into the regular classroom. Again, it is important for the regular classroom teacher to be aware of their needs and to consult with resource specialists concerning the recommended teaching methods. Preferential seating in the classroom should be provided to children who are hearing impaired.

Physical/Health Impaired

Children with orthopedic problems or with acute or chronic health conditions are included in this group. Some of these children are served in regular classrooms. Others may require special class placement or homebound instruction. The regular classroom teacher must be aware of the medical recommendations and of the limitations of the child imposed by the health condition.

Emotional Disturbance

Most school systems have specifically defined criteria for certifying a child as emotionally disturbed. Basically these children show very significant problems with behavior, affect, perception of reality, and interpersonal relationships over an extended period of time. The less seriously emotionally disturbed children may be served in regular classrooms and may respond well to the structured behavior management techniques described in Chapters 4 and 5. Others may require alternative placements such as special classes, special schools, or 24-hour residential settings in order to best meet their needs.

Multihandicapped

Multihandicapped children exhibit combinations of handicaps such as deaf/blind or orthopedic/mental retardation. They are usually severely handicapped in some way. They frequently need help in providing for their very basic needs. A majority of these children are served in self-contained special-education settings rather than mainstreamed into regular classrooms.

Autism

In the past, autistic children were often included under the category of emotionally disturbed. Autism is now defined as a developmental disability. Children who are diagnosed as autistic show a pervasive lack of normal social responsiveness, gross deficits in communication and associated features that may include resistance to change, oddities of movement, self-stimulation, attachments to inanimate objects, and unusual responses to sensory stimuli. These children often require self-contained classroom settings although higher-functioning autistic children may be served in a regular classroom.

Intellectually Gifted

The intellectually gifted are defined as exceptional children under the law due to their superior intellectual abilities and their potential for academic achievement. In most cases, children who are selected to participate in special school programs for the gifted and talented exhibit an IQ score of 130 or above on standardized intelligence testing (Horowitz & O'Brien, 1986). This definition, however, neglects other factors such as specific talents or creativity and provides only one measure of giftedness. Some school systems consider factors such as achievement or creative output in deciding which students should be placed in gifted programs. The ultimate goal of gifted programs is to help these students realize their superior potential and contribute as much as possible to society.

Some gifted children are best served in a regular classroom with modifications. Others may require special education programming due to their advancement. These children are usually verbally proficient and have a superior memory. They may also be skeptical of what they are told and may have good powers of critical thinking. They have good abstract-thinking skills, look for cause-effect relationships and may be creative when solving problems. Due to their superior cognitive ability, they are often easily bored in a regular classroom, and this boredom can be misinterpreted by teachers as lack of cooperation or as dislike of the teacher or the class. They may disdain routine and drill. For many of these children, social skills have not kept pace with cognitive and academic development and they may be socially inept. Some may exhibit attention-getting behavior or produce low-quality work in an attempt to meet their social needs.

Self-perceptions of Gifted Students

What do gifted students think about being labeled as gifted? To find out, Guskin, Okolo, Zimmerman and Peng (1986) administered questionnaires to 295 academically gifted and artistically talented students, ages 9–15, who were attending summer programs for gifted and talented youths. Results indicated that these gifted and talented students viewed themselves favorably and they reported receiving favorable treatment from others. Generally these gifted and talented students believed that giftedness is attained by working hard and that they, as a group, are not that different from other students. While these students did not report peer rejection, they recognized the potential for such action if gifted students are considered elite. The study suggests that gifted and talented students, perhaps for social reasons, may want to view giftedness as resulting from personal effort rather than from an inborn ability.

Programs for the gifted are varied. They may include enrichment activities within the regular classroom or acceleration to a higher-level class. Acceleration may happen at any stage of a student's academic career from kindergarten to college. Some gifted students are grouped with other gifted students for instruction in selected subjects while maintaining contact with students in a regular classroom for other activities. For example, they may take mini-courses, be placed in honors classes, or attend special classes during vacation periods. Gifted students have much to offer in their classrooms and ultimately to society. The task of the regular classroom teacher as well as other teachers is to help develop these students' potential to the fullest.

Some Problems Require Referral

Identifying special-needs children is not automatic. You may be the first person to recognize the need to refer a child for special services. Although you have the primary responsibility for dealing with problems that arise in your classroom, students may have serious problems that will not change as a result of your efforts. These problems can range from poor health to poor home conditions. Students with serious emotional problems who cannot relate properly in the classroom can create management difficulties and interfere with the education of other students. At other times, normal students may engage in excessively disruptive behavior that you cannot change without careful planning. Success in teaching basic academic skills may well depend on whether problems such as these are remedied.

A student should be referred to a resource specialist for problems that you cannot correct and that are interfering with academic achievement and personal development. Teachers should not assume that someone else has already sought or will seek proper assistance. When in doubt about referrals, you should consult with resource professionals. Together, you can then determine whether the student should be seen directly by a specialist.

Problems that may require referral to a resource professional generally fall into seven categories: health-related; visual; hearing; learning; behavioral/emotional; speech; and home-related. We will discuss each category and indicate specific behavior that might lead you to consider referral to a resource specialist.

Health-related Problems

Health-related problems are often unrecognized as the cause of poor academic achievement. Physical difficulties can impair students' performance regardless of their intellectual capacity. Poor health can also affect a student's social behavior. Very often, an irritable, inattentive, or apathetic child is labeled immature or unmotivated, and the causes of this behavior are not investigated by the teacher or the parents. Health problems may occur in any classroom but are especially prevalent in school districts that serve a large proportion of students from low socioeconomic backgrounds. Behavior management techniques cannot successfully overcome problems related to poor health.

Teachers should be aware of subtle behavior that students who have health-related problems sometimes exhibit. Acute medical conditions (e.g., vomiting, diarrhea) are easily recognizable, but other symptoms are less obviously medical and may appear to be attention-getting behavior. We have seen children who were originally labeled as "behavior problems" who were later diagnosed as having brain tumors or seizure disorders. Other health problems, such as inadequate nutrition, parasites, anemia, or lack of sleep, can affect a student's behavior in the classroom. Unless the cause of the problem is recognized, the behavior may be interpreted as lack of motivation or lack of interest in learning. Behavior problems are usually responsive to positive classroom management techniques, but poor behavior that stems from ill health is not.

Subtle signs that indicate that a student may need medical attention include:

1. Frequent complaints of headaches in the absence of other symptoms.
2. Lack of energy, appearing to "drag," or apathy regarding classroom activities.
3. Often falling asleep in class.
4. Irritable or hyperactive behavior.
5. Frequent stumbling or falling.
6. Sudden episodes of staring during which there is no response to classroom events.
7. Frequent absences due to illness.
8. Signs of drug abuse.

Occasionally, you will encounter a student who falsely complains of being sick. A teacher cannot always tell whether a child with physical complaints is malingering or if the symptoms are, in fact, real. A medical examination can either confirm or rule out the need for medical treatment. If the problem is found to be behavioral, classroom management techniques may be successful in effecting change.

Visual Problems

Students with visual problems may not pay attention or may disrupt classroom activities when board work is being completed. They may have difficulty with close work and activities that require fine visual-motor coordination, and therefore show little interest in these activities. Some visually impaired students have poor visual acuity: that is, they cannot see either distant or near objects clearly. Others have normal acuity, but may be unable to see objects in proper perspective. These students often have difficulty with printing and drawing activities. For example, they reverse letters and rotate designs, or they confuse letters that are similar (e.g., *b* and *d,* or *m,* and *w*). Students with these symptoms often have a visual-perception problem.

Other symptoms that should alert you to a student's need for an eye examination include (Willgoose, 1969):

1. Crossed, bloodshot, or swollen eyes; pus or sties around the eyes.
2. Complaints of headaches, dizziness, eye pain, nausea, blurred or double vision, or burning, itching eyelids. (Some of these symptoms can also be present with serious medical disorders unrelated to eye problems.)
3. Frequent stumbling or walking into objects. The student may not be able to accurately estimate the location of objects in space or may be unable to see objects that are not in the direct line of vision.
4. Inability to distinguish colors. (Some students may be colorblind.)
5. Holding reading material too close or too far away from the eyes. The student may also close one eye or squint when looking at objects. Rubbing of eyes may be frequent.
6. Inability to see distant objects that can readily be seen by others.
7. Undue sensitivity to light.

Vision screenings are sometime routinely administered to all students by the school nurse or a public-health nurse. You should make an effort to personally contact the parents of children whose screening indicates the need for a more complete examination. Parents occasionally postpone having their child's eyes checked because they lack the funds to pay for the examination. Teachers or school social workers can help the parents locate resources that will help provide for the examination.

Hearing Problems

Teachers frequently encounter students who "tune out" or do not pay attention to class discussions. Usually the problem is behavioral in nature and is responsive to classroom management techniques. However, poor hearing acuity is sometimes the cause of such behavior.

The presence of two or more of the following symptoms suggest the need for a hearing evaluation:

1. Failure to pay attention in class.
2. Facial expression indicating lack of comprehension when oral directions are given.
3. Mispronunciation of words.
4. Breathing only through the mouth.
5. Tendency to locate sound with one ear.
6. Unnatural voice pitch.
7. Complaints of earache; frequent ear rubbing.

As with vision screenings, an effort should be made to personally contact the parents of children whose tests indicate the need for a more complete examination.

Learning Problems

Most teachers have no difficulty recognizing students who do not learn as rapidly as others. Statements such as "Troy just can't seem to catch on" or "Rachel can't read even though she is in the fourth grade" are often made in response to students who fail to achieve at a level commensurate with their peers. Many of the students who fall behind academically exhibit undesirable behavior in school. They may fail to pay attention or disrupt the class during learning activities. They may fail to complete academic assignments. Some of these students may also be rejected by peers. When learning problems are present, work on social behavior alone will not insure that academic gains are made. It is possible to shape Troy into a very obedient child, but he still may not know how to read or subtract.

Students with learning problems require diagnostic testing to determine the major factors contributing to their poor academic performance. Some of these students have limited intellectual capacity. Others have normal learning ability, but do not achieve academically for other reasons. After the student has been evaluated, plans for remediation can be made. Determining the student's level of functioning and the specific skills that have been mastered is important. Inappropriate social behavior that occurs as a result of a student's inability to achieve academically may improve when a student is able to experience some success.

Behavioral and Emotional Problems

Students who frequently exhibit inappropriate behavior can easily tax a teacher's patience. Such children are often responding to environmental factors. For example, a student may receive peer approval or teacher attention for misconduct. These students usually respond well to the classroom management techniques described in Chapters 4 and 5. Sometimes, however, disruptive students fail to respond to the teacher. You should seek assistance if you are unable to control a student's disruptive behavior. Students who exhibit sudden and persistent changes in learning or behavior patterns may require an evaluation before a plan can be made to change their behavior.

Sometimes a student will act in a clearly inappropriate or even bizarre way. Such a student requires individual assistance from a specialist. The following behavior should alert you to the need for a referral:

1. Appears to be "out of contact." The student may be zombie-like in appearance or engrossed in a fantasy world.
2. Irrelevant or bizarre talk. Occasionally, you will find a student who is echolalic (a person who pathologically echoes the speech of others). Speech may be infantile.
3. Apparent aversion to people. The student may withdraw, seek isolation, or fail to communicate with others.
4. Self-mutilation. For example, the student may continually pick and scratch body parts.
5. Continual rocking, finger wiggling, and extreme fascination with spinning objects.
6. Repetitive behavior (the student exhibits the same behavior over and over again).
7. Extremely aggressive or violent behavior.
8. Antisocial behavior, such as lying or stealing.

9. Inability to concentrate or to remain still for more than a few seconds at a time.
10. Excessively fearful or suspicious behavior.

Speech Problems

Students who are unable to pronounce words clearly or who stutter are sometimes mimicked and teased by their peers. Other students may have communication problems that are not as readily apparent but that interfere with their academic performance. For example, they may be unable to remember names of objects or to put events in a logical order.

Referral to a specialist should be considered when the student exhibits the following difficulties in communication (Zaslow, 1974):

1. Frequent misarticulation of words. The student may be difficult to understand.
2. Stuttering.
3. Abnormal voice quality. The student may have a very nasal or hoarse voice.
4. Inability to remember common words. The student may gesture and say ''thing'' or ''stuff'' in place of common words.
5. Tangential or irrelevant conversation.
6. Inability to follow oral directions.
7. Difficulty with tasks, such as sequencing problems or stories.
8. Frequent grammatical errors incommensurate with age.
9. Difficulty in remembering what to say after raising hand in class. The student may appear to understand a process and then forget it or be unable to apply it to a different situation.

Giftedness

Gifted children frequently come to the attention of teachers through a history of outstanding grades in the academic areas. Teachers may also be alerted to the need for referral by a child's superior score on a group-ability test or on standardized achievement tests. Students who complete especially creative projects in writing, science, or other subject areas, and whose expressed ideas are above expectation based on age and grade, are also candidates for testing to determine eligibility for a gifted program.

The gifted student may not necessarily be the top student in the class academically. Due to boredom and lack of motivation, some gifted students achieve well below potential level. The teacher should be alert to subtle signs of giftedness and suggest testing for those children who may be lower-achieving gifted students. It is better for teachers to over-refer than to miss students who may need special instruction to develop their superior talents.

Home-related Problems

All children do not live in an adequate home environment. Many are deprived, both economically and emotionally. Some children are the victims of intentional neglect. In other cases, the parents may simply be unable to provide for their children. As a result, a student may be unkempt, improperly clothed, malnourished, and constantly sick. Lack of heat or irregular meals may be reported. Frequent absences from school are common. Children who are neglected or deprived are usually unable to perform at their potential level in school. A resource professional, such as a social worker, must often intervene and assist the family in obtaining needed resources and in improving the home environment.

In addition to living in a deprived environment, some children are the victims of abuse. This fact should be recognized by all educators. Child abuse may involve physical maltreatment, emotional maltreatment, sexual abuse, and neglect. In the past few years, the wide prevalence of child sexual abuse has become more apparent to social-service professionals and to educators.

Specialists have attributed the increased reports of sexual abuse to both a greater awareness concerning the problem as well as more frequency of abuse (Gratz, Maddock, Larson, & Gentry, 1986). Child sexual abuse includes a range of activities from fondling, to actual intercourse, to viewing of pornographic materials with a child (Irwin, 1986). Educators should be alert to signs of possible sexual abuse and follow through to protect the child following voluntary disclosure.

Behavior in children that may be indicative of sexual abuse includes (Sgroi, 1982):

1. Above average sexual knowledge for age.
2. Overly mature behavior.
3. Hints about sexual activity or inappropriate sexual play with toys or peers.

4. Seductive behavior.
5. Depression.
6. Lack of trust, especially with significant others.
7. Drops in academic performance.
8. Difficulty in concentrating.
9. Overly aggressive or overly compliant behavior and poor peer relationships.

This list is not inclusive. You are encouraged to consult Sgroi (1982), Vevier and Tharinger (1986), or other materials for in-depth discussions of sexual abuse and its signs.

Child abuse is not restricted to any socioeconomic level: It occurs in all social classes. All states have now passed laws that require the reporting of abuse or suspected abuse. In some states, failure to report can result in legal action against the person who has knowledge of, or suspects, abuse. It is important to remember that you do not have to have absolute proof of abuse. If abuse is suspected, it should be reported. The agency handling abuse in the state will make the investigation to determine whether further intervention is warranted. Some states ensure the confidentiality of reports. Failure to immediately report an incident of child abuse may endanger the child's life and will delay needed professional assistance to the parents.

Warning Signs

A child's appearance, reports of inhumane treatment, and behavior may all signal that a child is being mistreated. The American Humane Society (1971) has developed the following indicators that can alert teachers that a child may need help:

PHYSICAL APPEARANCE

- *Does the child have bruises or abrasions, suspicious burns, cigarette burns, or bite marks? Are the injuries repeated, located on unlikely parts of the body, or inadequately explained?*
- *Does the child show evidence of medical neglect? Does he or she need dental care, glasses, or treatment for a medical condition such as impetigo?*

- *Is the child malnourished? Does he or she come to school without breakfast or go without lunch?*
- *Does the child wear adequate clothing for the weather? Is the clothing well cared for? Is the child dirty?*
- *Does the child appear listless, tired, or fall asleep in class?*

BEHAVIOR

- *Does the child display aggressive, disruptive, or destructive behavior in school?*
- *Does the child display withdrawn, passive, or excessively compliant behavior? Does he or she have a low self-image?*
- *Does the child habitually come to school much too early or hang around after school?*
- *Does the child frequently fail to come to school or exhibit chronic tardiness?*

Emotional Abuse at School

Most of the literature pertaining to child abuse has dealt with abuse by parents. However, a new clinical entity, emotional abuse at school, has been reported in the pediatric literature. Krugman and Krugman (1984) describe a case history of 17 children who showed signs of emotional abuse as a result of their classroom experiences. Subjected to a teacher who labeled them stupid, verbally harassed them, and threatened them with harm, the children developed anxiety, negative self-images, and began to worry excessively. They also reported that they feared their teachers. The children became quiet and complacent in the classroom but were visibly upset at home. The personality changes occurred within two weeks of being placed in a class with an erratic teacher. The symptoms disappeared within two weeks after the teacher was replaced.

Emotional abuse is no doubt inflicted on students by some teachers. The effects of such abuse on students who are subjected to it for a full school year can be devastating. Psychological maltreatment can take many forms including emotional abuse, emotional neglect, and mental cruelty (Hart & Brassard, 1987). Psychological abuse may be more prevalent and potentially more harmful than other forms of child abuse, and neglect in particular is perhaps the most insidious of all (Hart & Brassard, 1987).

Mainstreaming the Exceptional Child

The term "mainstreaming" is used by many educators to describe any integration of exceptional children into regular classrooms. For some educators, mainstreaming includes placing exceptional children with their nonhandicapped peers for lunch, recess, music, and art while returning them to a self-contained classroom for academic instruction.

Other educators use more definite parameters when applying this strategy. MacMillan, Jones, and Meyers (1976) suggest the following conditions be met when mainstreaming: (a) the exceptional child should be enrolled in a regular classroom and spend at least half of his or her time there; (b) the regular-class teacher should be primarily responsible for developing a program for the child and should be accountable for his or her progress; (c) no categorical labels such as mental retardation should be applied to the mainstreamed child. Mainstreaming should be limited to those situations where appropriate educational strategies can be applied in a regular setting.

This definition is rather stringent and does not describe the situation in many schools. MacMillan, Jones, and Meyers (1976) are concerned with the instructional aspect of mainstreaming while other educators use the mainstreaming concept to provide social experiences for exceptional children. Regardless of the parameters applied to the mainstreaming approach, it has become an integral part of special education services in school systems throughout the nation.

Mainstreaming: Hints for Teachers

1. *Schedule a meeting with the special education teacher who is familiar with the child to discuss the child's strong points and weaker areas. Also, find out what behavior management techniques have proven successful in dealing with social and/or behavioral problems.*
2. *Obtain background data on the child to learn of problems that could interfere with the child's adjustment to the classroom. For example, does the child have hearing problems and need preferential seating?*
3. *Review the most recent educational test results on the child and complete baseline educational testing in your classroom to determine the child's specific skills and deficits.*

4. *Adapt instructional activities in the classroom to allow the student to experience success.*
5. *Enlist the aid of other students for peer tutoring if needed.*
6. *Allow the child to participate in all classroom activities, but gear your expectations to the child's capability.*
7. *Explore opportunities for using mainstreaming as a learning experience for other students.*
8. *Use positive reinforcement techniques in dealing with mainstreamed children.*
9. *Provide the child ample opportunities for success through use of techniques such as behavior shaping.*
10. *In thinking about the mainstreamed child, consider the child's strengths and let these overshadow the deficits.*
11. *Approach the mainstreaming experience with positive expectations that it will work out well.*
12. *Enjoy having the child in your class!*

Academic Aspects of Mainstreaming

As an educational approach, mainstreaming is effective in working with handicapped pupils. Based on a review and analysis of 11 empirical studies of mainstreaming during the period of 1975 to 1984, Wang and Baker (1985–86) concluded that mainstreamed disabled students consistently outperformed nonmainstreamed disabled students with comparable classifications. Mainstreaming procedures may vary depending on the nature of the child's handicap and the resources of the school.

Children with learning disorders such as mild mental retardation, borderline intelligence, and learning disabilities usually spend the bulk of their day in a regular classroom. Visually handicapped and hearing impaired children may also spend much of their time in a regular class. These students may receive some remedial instruction from a resource teacher, but most of the academic instruction can be provided by the classroom teacher.

Many exceptional children have difficulty competing academically with the nonhandicapped children. Some eventually exhibit a significant academic lag and find it impossible to satisfactorily complete most of the grade-level work. A 12-year-old who is reading at the third-grade level cannot complete assignments in content areas such as history, geography, or science from texts written at the sixth-grade level. The same student may also have problems in arithmetic due to inability to read the instructions. Many of these students may be able to understand and remember the material if the text assignments are read to them, but will fail if alternative teaching methods are not used.

Regular classroom teachers must remain alert to the needs of the mainstreamed child if the academic experiences of the child are to be successful. Admittedly, this is difficult when a teacher has responsibility for a large class of other children. However, the skill levels of normal children also vary and skill-grouping may also work to the advantage of the nonhandicapped children. The skill groups should be flexible to allow the students to move in and out of each group as needed. A handicapped child gains little emotional advantage by being mainstreamed and then labeled again by inflexible grouping as the slowest child in the class.

Teaching strategies such as reading texts aloud and giving tests orally may be of help to students who are reading well below grade level. Peer tutoring can often be used for this purpose and parents can be asked to tape record materials. Assignments should be individualized for those students, nonhandicapped as well as handicapped, who are below grade level in specific areas. One-to-one instruction will be needed to teach some basic concepts. Again, peer tutors or a teacher's aide can be helpful, but the regular teacher has the primary responsibility for the handicapped child's progress. These children should not be ignored by the teacher and left to the teacher's aide or peer tutors. All children should receive the benefit of the regular teacher's expertise and experience.

The same teaching techniques are not appropriate for all children who are mainstreamed into a regular classroom; however, some general guidelines may be helpful in working with most of these students:

1. Assignments should be broken down into small, manageable units that will provide the student with more immediate feedback and with frequent success experiences.
2. Directions should be simple and presented one at a time unless the student has demonstrated the ability to handle multiple directions. Modeling as well as verbal directions can be extremely beneficial for some children.
3. Previously learned skills should be reviewed and practiced regularly.

4. Distractions should be kept to a minimum. Some students may benefit from the use of study carrels when working on difficult assignments.
5. Students should be rewarded for successful completion of a task or task segment.

These general guidelines are also appropriate for teaching new skills to nonhandicapped students. It is suggested that they be incorporated into the daily teaching plans.

Academic Mainstreaming Review

1. *Determine the child's skill level*
2. *Be flexible with skill-grouping.*
3. *Use alternative teaching strategies such as reading texts aloud and giving tests orally.*
4. *Enlist the aid of peer tutors.*
5. *Break assignments into small, manageable units to provide immediate feedback and frequent success experiences.*
6. *Keep directions simple.*
7. *Present directions one at a time unless the student has demonstrated an ability to handle multiple directions.*
8. *Review and practice previously learned skills regularly.*
9. *Keep distractions to a minimum.*
10. *Supplement verbal directions with modeling.*
11. *Reward successful completion of tasks or task segments.*
12. *Provide the student with a study carrel when assignments are difficult.*

The school-resource teacher can assist teachers as well as students. For children with very specialized needs, such as the hearing or visually impaired, the resource teacher can provide materials and suggestions for maximizing the students' educational experiences. Do not hesitate to request the expertise of school specialists in dealing with problems in the classroom. Consultation with specialists will add to your own expertise and will better equip you for dealing with similar problems in the future.

As Teachers See Them

Do teachers perceive and treat all students equitably in a mainstreamed classroom? Campbell, Dobson, and Bost (1985), in a study of 105 educators, found that various educators rated behavior problems of mentally retarded students as less serious than the same behavior problems of nonhandicapped or physically handicapped pupils. They also recommended more authoritarian treatments for the nonhandicapped than for the physically handicapped. Educators may expect more behavior problems from the mentally retarded, but they also judge the seriousness of these problems on the basis of whether the student has the ability to "know better."

Campell, Dobson, and Bost (1985) postulate that behavior problems of students in mainstreamed classrooms may be caused by educators' failure to internalize strategies for teaching a diverse group of students. These researchers suggest that educators acquire skills for dealing with the behavior problems of all students, handicapped and nonhandicapped, in an equitable and appropriate way.

Social Aspects of Mainstreaming

The academic requirements of some handicapped children cannot be met in the regular classroom due to their handicaps and their specialized instructional needs. However, children who have the ability to participate in regular classroom activities will benefit from the experience of being part of a larger group. Even limited classroom integration provides these children with opportunities to learn from the other children through modeling and exposes them to the types of situations and interactions that are required for success outside the special education classroom. These children are not sheltered once they leave the school, and mainstreaming provides them with opportunities to learn to manage in a normal environment.

Unfortunately, special education pupils are not always well accepted by other students. Some may be ostracized, and this can contribute to low self-esteem and lack of self-confidence. Others may be teased and ridiculed by their classmates. Research (Luftig, 1988; Zetlin & Murtaugh, 1988) has found that mainstreamed, mentally retarded students report greater feelings of loneliness and isolation from others than do their nonretarded peers and that they have fewer and less stable friendships.

Some exceptional students are accepted but "babied" by other students to the extent that, unless the teacher is vigilant, they may begin to totally rely on the help of the other students. None of these situations is desirable. The goal of the classroom teacher is to promote healthy peer relationships in which the exceptional student is accepted as a worthwhile person who has something to contribute to others.

Teachers may want to develop instructional units on handicapping conditions as well as on feelings and emotions that are shared by handicapped people. This can increase the probability of successfully mainstreaming the exceptional student into the classroom. It is also important to increase the social skills and personal independence of the handicapped child. Jenkins, Speltz, and Odom (1985) found that mainstreaming alone did not accelerate development of handicapped children. These authors suggested that detailed curricula to structure the interactions between the handicapped and nonhandicapped pupils are needed to produce positive changes. Beckman and Kohl (1987) suggest that positive interactions and increased play behavior may favor the nonhandicapped in integrated free-play settings.

Promoting Understanding and Acceptance of Handicaps

Difficulty accepting peers who are different is not limited to normal children. Even handicapped children may not accept children with handicaps that are different from their own. Israelson (1980) reports on a project used in a classroom of deaf children to sensitize them to the orthopedic handicap of a new student as well as to other students with handicaps different from their own. The project was begun after an orthopedically handicapped and deaf child, who was placed in the classroom, was met with derision, taunting, exclusion from games, and physical violence.

Group counseling and instructional units were unsuccessful in minimizing the derision toward the new child; however, a mini-unit on a number of handicapping conditions including blindness, deafness, deaf-blindness, and physical impairments was successful. The unit was unique in that students were given materials that allowed them to simulate different types of handicaps and were asked to go about their daily tasks during each simulation phase. For example, a blindfold was used to simulate blindness while homemade splints and bandages were used to incapacitate hands or legs for the orthopedic phase. In addition to the simulation experiences, students read books and saw films related to a variety of handicapping conditions. Emphasis was also placed on role playing to teach ways of helping people with handicaps. The unit proved worthwhile in creating an empathic emotional environment in the deaf-education classroom.

Behavioral Aspects of Mainstreaming

To a large extent, the teacher's success or failure in managing the academic and social aspects of mainstreaming will be reflected in the child's behavior in the classroom. Children who are neglected academically and who lag behind the other children often exhibit attention-getting behavior or obstinate behavior, or act out frustrations in the classroom. The child who is socially ostracized may display similar problems. Failure to deal adequately with the academic and social needs of the mainstreamed child thus compounds the problems for the teacher.

Any approach to behavioral remediation must initially consider whether the child's academic and social needs are being met adequately. The structured behavior management techniques discussed in Chapters 4 and 5 are appropriate for dealing with the behavior of handicapped as well as nonhandicapped children. We suggest that you concentrate on the use of positive strategies and employ negative means only when absolutely necessary. These children must deal with many negative events in their lives. Their emotional development would benefit if their classroom experience could be a positive one.

Some modifications of the behavior change techniques will be necessary when using them with learning-impaired children, especially mentally retarded children. Rewards will need to be provided more frequently because these children may not be able to remember the connection between a behavior and its consequences if the reward is deferred. More frequent rewards also provide feedback in teaching and reinforcing new skills, a necessary ingredient when teaching new concepts to the learning impaired.

Rules should be simple and clear and should be reviewed periodically. Due to memory impairments, some children may break a rule because they have forgotten it. Contracts should be short and written in simple terms. The point system may be too abstract for some students and more concrete rewards such as stars may be necessary. The use of behavior-shaping techniques may help these students learn to attend to tasks for longer periods of time.

Giving the student some responsibility and status that is commensurate with ability may help promote appropriate behavior. Handicapped children can be line leaders; they can be teachers' helpers in watering the plants; and they can take up homework assignments. Remember that they should receive some of the special duties in the classroom.

On occasion, you may encounter mainstreamed children whose behavior is very difficult for you to manage. In such cases, consult with the school counselor or the school psychologist. These professionals may observe the class, assist in setting up a classroom management plan, monitor the effectiveness of the plan, and suggest modifications when necessary. Most counselors and school psychologists would be hesitant to offer services, however, unless the request is initiated by the teacher.

Those children who exhibit a true attention-deficit disorder are usually extremely difficult to manage behaviorally, even with consultative help. Some of these children may require pharmacological management in combination with behavior management. Those very distractible, very active children who do not respond to your consistent behavior management efforts may be helped by a referral to their pediatrician. This referral can be made by the parents following a conference with the teacher. The pediatrician should be provided with an accurate description of the child's behavior to assist in the overall medical assessment. The behavior management program used in the classroom should not be discontinued if the child is placed on medicine. Medicine is not magic. While medicine may help a child who has attention deficits, structured behavior management techniques will also be needed to maximize success.

Mainstreaming has worked very well for many children. The attention educators are giving to this aspect of programming for exceptional students can pay big dividends in the student's adaptation to both school and community.

Summary

The main provisions of the Education for All Handicapped Children Act have ensured the right of these students to a full and equal education.

With mainstreaming, teachers can meet the needs of the exceptional child in the regular classroom. Teachers should also be aware of the types of specialized services available in their school and should refer students with special needs for remedial assistance. It is important for teachers to recognize signs that can indicate the need for referral to a specialist outside of the class, or even outside of the school.

Resource specialists can contribute a great deal to the development of students who require their services; however, the regular classroom teacher has the primary responsiblility for most exceptional students. Teachers must develop strategies for successfully mainstreaming the exceptional child into the regular classroom. Given the coordinated efforts of resource personnel and the regular classroom teacher, handicapped children should have a successful academic experience.

CHECKLIST OF REFERRAL INDICATORS

Area	Signs to look for	Yes	No	Comments
Health-related	1. Frequent complaints of headaches, stomachaches, or other somatic symptoms. 2. Lack of energy; apathy; appears to "drag." 3. Often falls asleep in class. 4. Frequent stumbling or falling. 5. Episodes of staring during which there is no response to classroom events. 6. Frequent absences due to illness. 7. Suspected alcohol or drug abuse.			
Vision	1. Failure to pay attention to board work. 2. Problems with fine-motor coordination. 3. Crossed, bloodshot, or swollen eyes.			

Area	Signs to look for	Yes	No	Comments
Vision (cont.)	4. Complaints of headaches, dizziness, eye pain, nausea, blurred or double vision, or burning or itching eyes. 5. Frequent walking into objects or stumbling. 6. Inability to distinguish colors. 7. Holding reading materials too close or too far away. 8. Closing one eye or squinting. 9. Frequent rubbing of eyes. 10. Inability to see distant objects clearly. 11. Undue sensitivity to light.			
Hearing	1. Failure to pay attention in class. 2. Facial expression indicating lack of comprehension when oral directions are given. 3. Mispronunciation of words. 4. Breathing exclusively through the mouth. 5. Tendency to localize sound with one ear. 6. Unnatural voice pitch.			

Area	Signs to look for	Yes	No	Comments
Hearing (cont.)	7. Complaints of earache; frequent ear rubbing.			
Learning Problems	1. Disruptive behavior. 2. Excessive shyness. 3. Social withdrawal. 4. Poor peer relationships. 5. Perseverative behavior. 6. Excessively fearful or suspicious behavior. 7. Antisocial behavior such as lying or stealing. 8. Inability to concentrate or to remain still for more than a few minutes. 9. Extremely aggressive or violent behavior. 10. Excessive self-stimulating behavior. 11. Self-mutilation behavior. 12. Irrelevant or bizarre talk; echolalia; infantile speech. 13. Appears to be "out of contact."			
Giftedness	1. History of excellent grades in academic work. 2. Superior work on special projects such as creative writing, science projects, social studies projects, etc.			

Area	Signs to look for	Yes	No	Comments
Giftedness (cont.)	3. Awards for outstanding work in academic areas (e.g., math award). 4. Superior test scores (academic and intellectual). 5. Above-average insight or quality of ideas in relation to chronological level. 6. Disruptive behavior.			
Home-related (Child Abuse)	1. Bruises, abrasions, suspicious burns, cigarette burns, bite marks that are located on unlikely parts of the body or are inadequately explained. 2. Repeated injuries. 3. Evidence of medical neglect (i.e., needs dental care, glasses, or treatment for a medical condition.) 4. Malnourishment. The child comes to school without breakfast or goes without lunch. 5. Inadequate clothing for the weather. Poor grooming. 6. Listless or tired behavior. Child falls asleep in class. 7. Aggressive, disruptive, or destructive behavior in school.			

Area	Signs to look for	Yes	No	Comments
Home-related (cont.)	8. Withdrawn, passive, or excessively compliant behavior. 9. Frequent absences or chronic tardiness. 10. Tendency to come to school much too early or to hang around after school. 11. Above-average sexual knowledge for age. 12. Overly-mature behavior. 13. Hints about sexual activity. 14. Inappropriate sexual play with toys or peers. 15. Seductive behavior. 16. Depression. 17. Lack of trust toward adults, especially significant others. 18. Drop in academic performance. 19. Difficulty with concentration. 20. Overly aggressive or compliant behavior. 21. Poor peer relationships.			

References

American Humane Society. (1971). *Guidelines for schools.*

Beckman, P. J., & Kohl, F. L. (1987). Interactions of preschoolers with and without handicaps in integrated and segregated settings: A longitudinal study. *Mental Retardation, 25,* 5–11.

Brown, A., & Campione, J. (1986). Psychological theory and the study of learning disabilities. *American Psychologist, 41,* 1059–1068.

Campbell, N., Dobson, J., & Bost, J. (1985). Educator perceptions of behavior problems of mainstreamed students. *Exceptional children, 51,* 298–303.

Education for All Handicapped Children Act of 1975 — (Public Law No. 94–142) 20 U.S.C. 1145 (1986). §§ 1401 et seq.

Education of the Handicapped Act. Amendment of 1986 (Public Law No. 99–457) 100 STAT 1145 (1986).

Gratz, Y., Maddock, J., Larson, N., & Gentry, C. (1986). Conference: Annual Treatment Conference on Sexual Abuse, Hilton Head, SC.

Grossman, H. J. (Ed.) (1983). *Manual on terminology and classification in mental retardation.* Washington: American Association on Mental Deficiency.

Guskin, S., Okolo, C., Zimmerman, E., & Peng, C. (1986). Being labeled gifted or talented: Meanings and effects perceived by students in special programs. *Gifted Child Quarterly, 30,* 61–64.

Hart, S. N., & Brassard, M. R. (1987). A major threat to children's mental health: Psychological maltreatment. *American Psychologist, 42,* 160–165.

Horowitz, F., & O'Brien, M. (1986). Gifted and talented children: State of knowledge and directions for reseach. *American Psychologist, 41,* 1147–1152.

Irwin, S. (1986). The reality of sexual abuse in children. *The Tennessee School Psychologist, 3,* 3, 7–8

Israelson, J. (1980). I'm special too — a classroom promotes understanding and acceptance of handicaps. *Teaching Exceptional Children, 46,* 35–47.

Jenkins, J. R., Speltz, M. L., & Odom, S. L. (1985). Integrating normal and handicapped preschoolers: Effects on child development and social interaction. *Exceptional Children, 52,* 7–17.

Krugman, R. D., & Krugman, M. K. (1984). Emotional abuse in the classroom; the pediatrician's role in diagnosis and treatment. *American Journal of Diseases of Children, 138,* 284–286.

Luftig, R. L. (1988). Assessement of the perceived school loneliness and isolation of mentally retarded and nonretarded students. *American Journal on Mental Retardation. 92,* 472–475.

MacMillan, D. L., Jones, R. L., & Meyers, C. E. (1976). Mainstreaming the mildly retarded: Some questions, cautions and guidelines. *Mental Retardation, 14,* 3–10.

Sgroi, S. (1982). *A handbook of clinical intervention in child sexual abuse.* Lexington, KY: Lexington Books.

Tennessee Department of Education. (1982). *Student evaluation manual.*

Vevier, E., & Tharinger, D. (1986). Child sexual abuse: A review and intervention framework for the school psychologist. *Journal of School Psychology, 24,* 293–311.

Wang, M., & Baker, E. (1985–1986). Mainstreaming programs: Design features and effects. *Journal of Special Education, 19,* 503–521.

Willgoose, C. E. (1969). *Health Education in the Elementary School.* Philadelphia: W. B. Saunders.

Zaslow, E. L. (1974). The speech pathologist. *Today's Education, 63,* 27–29.

Zetlin, A. G., & Murtaugh, M. (1988). Friendship patterns of mildly learning handicapped and nonhandicapped high school students. *American Journal on Mental Retardation, 92,* 447–454.

CHAPTER 8

Right and Wrong: Ethical and Legal Problems of Classroom Management

"Julia, you seem so jittery. What's wrong?"

"Don't you know? I'm being evaluated today. I expect I'll have observers in my classroom most of the day. It will be my luck for everything to go wrong."

Teacher accountability and teacher evaluation are issues that are becoming increasingly important to educators and to the general public. Many teachers consider it prudent to carry insurance to protect themselves from lawsuits arising from their actions in the classroom. Students' rights also remain an issue of critical concern. Now, more than ever, teachers need to be aware of the legal and ethical issues inherent in managing a classroom. In this chapter, we will examine some of the ethical and legal aspects of classroom control. Issues pertaining to accountability and teacher evaluation will also be discussed.

Ethical Issues: Behavior Change

The accepted goal of the educational process is to change behavior. Six-year-olds entering first grade have few academic skills, and they are socially immature. At the end of their public-school training, however, society expects them to exhibit advanced academic skills and mature and independent functioning. The entire schooling process, from grades 1–12, is directed toward this goal.

In recent years, new techniques have been developed to achieve desired behavior changes and, as a result, questions pertaining to the goals of behavior change have become more crucial. Several issues have been raised and debated in the professional literature. For example: are behavior management techniques being used merely to induce conformity; who should decide what kind of behavior should be changed; do teachers stifle creativity when students are required to conform to preconceived expectations?

In addition to issues pertaining to the goals of behavior change, questions have been raised about behavior change methodology. Is it ethical to use extrinsic or tangible rewards? When rewards are made contingent on desired behavior, is the process equal to bribery? Does a reward system teach undesirable values, for example, that desired aims can be bought? What are the long-range effects of providing tangible rewards? Other issues revolve around the use of negative behavior control techniques. Is it ethical to use criticism or corporal punishment to control students' behavior? What are the problems in using response cost or timeout? Should aversive methods be used in the classroom? These questions and others may arise in any consideration of classroom control. The resolution of these issues will be reflected in the goals set in the classroom and the methods used to reach them.

Purpose of Behavior Change

Traditionally, teachers have been considered successful when they are able to maintain a classroom where students sit quietly, refrain from talking to their neighbors, and raise their hands for permission to speak. The emphasis in recent years on informal education and open classrooms has changed this situation for some teachers. However, many principals still expect to see a quiet, well-controlled group of students when they patrol the halls or walk into a classroom.

Certainly, the question of whether behavior change techniques should be used to induce conformity must be taken seriously. We would agree with most educators that academic skills cannot be taught successfully when the classroom climate is utter chaos. A classroom environment must enable students to hear class discussions and to finish assigned seatwork without constant interruption; on the other hand, maintaining a quiet classroom sometimes becomes the primary goal. Students' mastery of academic and independent-thinking skills becomes secondary to their classroom demeanor. Sophisticated behavior control techniques have increased the teachers' ability to attain whatever goals they set in their classrooms. Consequently, the goals of behavior change become critically important.

There is controversy over who should set educational and behavioral goals for students. Society trusts that individuals will be prepared to set personal goals when they reach adulthood, but this may be an erroneous assumption. Some individuals need instruction in how to set goals. Most students are capable of much more self-direction than has been previously thought. If students are allowed the freedom to determine some of their own goals in school, they will be better prepared to set goals and manage their lives in adulthood.

The issue of student conformity versus independent behavior has not been satisfactorily resolved for many educators. Can a student who is being molded into a conforming adult by being expected to follow class rules also be encouraged to think independently on controversial issues and pursue independent research? We believe that stimulating ideas can be presented and independent-thinking skills can be established at the same time students are conforming to classroom rules. Few students who sit quietly in class behave in the same manner in other settings, such as at home or at play.

Students should not be shaped into docile beings who accept any rule without protest; students should be taught to discriminate between appropriate or inappropriate behavior for a particular setting. The primary emphasis in the classroom should be on learning and thinking. Behavior requirements should be developed in accordance with the type of skill being taught. Rules for rules' sake should be avoided.

Ethical and Legal Issues: Behavior Change Methodology

Historically, behavioral change techniques have been attacked on ethical grounds (Bentley, 1987). Ethical considerations related to classroom management often involve the methodology employed to effect the change. Both positive and negative techniques have been questioned. These questions are important and deserve serious consideration in any discussion of behavior change methodology. A teacher who has ethical reservations about a particular behavior change technique will probably not apply it. In this chapter, we will discuss some of the issues that have been raised and should be considered in making classroom decisions.

The use of behavior modification procedures in the classroom has not been specifically tested in court. Based on behavior modification cases in other settings, Wherry (1983) suggests that the following legal and ethical precautions be taken in using these procedures in the classroom: (a) individualize behavioral interventions; (b) obtain informed consent of the parent or guardian; (c) try behavioral strategies before placing a student in a more restrictive environment; (d) carefully document student progress and redesign ineffective interventions; and (e) limit the use of timeout and punishment procedures. Positive reward systems, timeout, and corporal punishment are most frequently used to change behavior in the classroom, and the morality of each of these approaches has been questioned.

Ethical Considerations Related to Positive Behavior Change Techniques

Positive behavior management techniques have been discussed in detail in Chapter 4. Essentially, the process provides a reward or payoff when a student exhibits desired behavior. The payment may be social, tangible, or may give the student some privilege. The student must perform the desired behavior in order to earn the reward.

The application of tangible reinforcers has raised an ethical question. Can the use of tangible rewards to change or maintain behavior be equated with bribery? O'Leary, Poulos, and Devine (1972) discuss in detail 11 major objections that have been raised against the use of tangible reinforcers to change behavior. These include concerns about whether receiving tangible rewards teaches students to use tangibles to control others and whether reward systems teach self-doubt by using "if-then" statements that imply the teacher doubts the student's ability to perform the behavior without a reward. A further concern focuses on the teacher who depends on token reinforcement: these teachers may come to rely on this form of behavior control and fail to develop other methods. Students who observe others being rewarded for appropriate behavior may begin to behave inappropriately in order to receive rewards for desirable behavior. Additional questions about tangible reinforcement relate to the duration of behavior change achieved, and to the effect of rewarding certain behavior over other behavior. A final objection suggests that tangible reinforcement may interfere with learning.

Reinforcement versus bribery. Different standards are applied to children than to adults. For example, as employed adults, we receive a payoff for performing the duties outlined in our job description. Most of us would be highly unlikely to continue our jobs if financial remuneration were suddenly discontinued. Are our employers bribing us to work? Are you being bribed to teach? Most of us would answer a resounding "NO!"

We feel that we are making honest and important contributions through our work.

On the other hand, outlining desired behavior for a child (for example: making the bed, picking up toys, completing homework, bringing books to class) and providing a tangible reward contingent on the desired behavior is often regarded as bribery. Expectations for children are sometimes higher than for adults. Just as work is usually not intrinsically rewarding enough for us to continue when external support (i.e., the paycheck) is withdrawn, so certain behavior required of children may not be inherently reinforcing. External support may be required until the behavior is well-established and is being maintained by intrinsic reinforcement. Careful study of classrooms that use tangible reinforcers indicates that rewards have been used to induce appropriate academic and social behavior in students.

Effects of tangible rewards on students. On the positive side, students will modify their behavior to receive rewards, and thus can learn new skills and function better in school. On the negative side, greed may inadvertently be taught and the student may imitate the teacher in attempting to control others through this method. Some students may attempt to manipulate the teacher by demanding rewards for continued good behavior.

For these reasons, tangible reinforcers should be used only when social or activity rewards are ineffective. When they are used, they should be paired with intangible reinforcers, such as praise. Fortunately, as people learn to perform new skills, the new behavior often becomes reinforcing in its own right, and extrinsic rewards are no longer required for it to be maintained.

Effects of tangible rewards on teachers. Certainly, finding that you can control another person's behavior through use of tangible rewards is potentially reinforcing. It is important, then, that teachers who use behavior change programs gradually diminish tangible rewards in favor of social reinforcement. Perhaps teachers should think of tangible rewards only as a temporary tool, and consider a self-monitoring program to determine the extent to which their classroom behavior change program continues to rely on tangible reinforcement. No teacher wants to fall into the trap of using tangible rewards simply because the system is reinforcing this behavior. As with all classroom management systems, the ultimate aim is to help the students.

Effects of tangible rewards on nonrewarded students. The effects of giving tangible rewards to some students and not to others must also be considered. When children who are not rewarded see one or more of their peers receiving rewards for performing a particular behavior, they may feel that the situation is unfair.

Teacher's Helper

Jamie was a chronic dawdler who usually did not finish her assigned work without nagging and prompts from Ms. Mansouri, her teacher. Finally, Ms. Mansouri decided to reduce the nagging and reward speed in Jamie by allowing her to run errands and perform other "teacher's helper" tasks when she finished her work. This tactic worked very well for Jamie, but to Ms. Mansouri's surprise, other students also began completing their work more quickly so that they could be helpers. Ms. Mansouri found it necessary to develop a list of "helper tasks" in order to reward other students in her class.

In this example, it is clear that Ms. Mansouri had stumbled on a very effective reward for several of her students. It was important in this case that she reward the efforts of other students as well as Jamie. Otherwise, the behavior of the students may have deteriorated. In a classroom setting, one student cannot be singled out for special attention without creating problems with other students. Classroom contracts, discussed in Chapter 9, offer one alternative to circumvent this problem by allowing students to pursue independent alternatives and still receive a reward.

Effects of unnatural rewards. In general, behavior supported by reinforcers that are unnatural to the situation (for example, tokens) may fall off when the external support is withdrawn. A teacher who proposes the use of tangible reinforcement must make an effort to develop more natural reinforcers, such as social attention, if the behavior change is to be of long duration.

Legal Considerations Related to Positive Reward Systems

The use of positive rewards has legal implications. You should insure that students are not made to perform for privileges they are entitled to as a right. For example, John may certainly be motivated to earn the privilege of eating his lunch, but the right to eat is basic and denying such a right can have legal implications. It is better that he be allowed to earn a bag of potato chips as an extra treat and that his basic meal not be contingent on behavior. To quote Martin (1975). "If the program leads to a severe change in status or if personal property is taken away and used as a reward to be earned, it may violate the Fifth Amendment'' (p. 126). Teachers should question the practice of confiscating students' property for the purpose of returning it when the student has met a certain behavioral or academic standard.

Ethical Considerations Related to Negative Behavior Change Techniques

Ethical questions also surround the use of negative techniques for changing behavior. Two negative techniques in particular have traditionally been accepted for controlling behavior in the classroom: criticism and corporal punishment. Two additional methods are being used with increasing frequency: timeout and response cost. We have already discussed the use of these strategies in Chapter 5, but we want to reconsider them in light of the ethical and legal questions they pose for teachers. The major ethical issue related to negative techniques for changing behavior is whether negative approaches should be used at all. Is it wrong to punish a child? To answer this question educators must make a value judgement.

Corporal punishment. The use of corporal punishment in American schools goes back to the Puritan settlement of the Massachusetts Bay Colony (Piele, 1978). It is a well-established means of discipline in schools. Yet, the question of who should decide what behavior should be discouraged is seldom asked before it is used. Perhaps the relatively short-term effectiveness of this technique has resulted in complacency. Further, corporal punishment is often employed without prior planning. Regardless of how it is used, the teacher should remember that behavior change techniques are not meant to foster subservience or conformity. A teacher who paddles a child for talking during class periods or who spanks a child who talks back is communicating values loudly and clearly.

Educators in school districts that allow corporal punishment must ask whether teachers have a right to inflict pain and humiliation on other human beings. Certainly, most of us would refrain from doing so to an adult. In the case of a child, however, corporal punishment is justified by statements such as: ''the child will learn to behave'' or ''whipping is good for the child.'' Adults who spank or hit to punish are modeling aggressive behavior for children, and children tend to imitate behavior that they have seen modeled. Children who are abused by their parents often grow up to abuse their own children. Furthermore, the use of corporal punishment may engender strong emotional reactions in children. Children who are repeatedly punished physically may suffer emotional problems. Children who are made to feel inconsequential will suffer from low self-esteem.

As we just mentioned, adults tend to refrain from physically striking other adults. However, inflicting pain on others may continue in a different form. Criticism, sarcasm, and verbal downgrading of others result in emotional pain for the recipient. It is possible that the negative events that are suffered in childhood are imitated, in perhaps a different and more acceptable form, in adulthood.

Other questions you should ask yourself about the use of corporal punishment include: (a) is this child entitled to the same rights as adults; (b) what am I teaching this child by a spanking; (c) will the child refrain from misconduct as a result of this punishment or learn that one can do as one pleases when big enough to exert power over others; (d) how will this child react emotionally to paddling; (e) will this child develop a dislike for me or, more seriously, for school itself. Behavior theorists postulate that repeated incidents of physical punishment at school could result in such reaction. No conscientious teacher would want this to occur.

Criticism. Criticism is commonly used for changing behavior, but teachers seldom raise ethical questions about this method of behavioral control. Not all teachers and parents are constructive in the use of criticism. For example, criticism is sometimes used without giving thought to the overall effect it can have on the child. It is not unusual to hear a teacher say "Martin is a lazy child. He could do better if he tried," or "Kate, you are a sloppy writer. You must learn to be neater." Most teachers who use criticism to change behavior are quick to point out that they only use constructive criticism. The term "constructive criticism," however, is often used to cover criticism in general.

Ginott (1965) defines "constructive criticism" as criticism that is confined to the target behavior and that omits negative remarks about personality. For example, a teacher might say, "Kate, papers are easier to read when they're neatly copied." Such a statement provides information regarding the task to be completed, and it casts no aspersions on the recipient. Or a teacher might say, "Martin, in order to complete your arithmetic assignments on time, it will be necessary for you to work during study time rather than look at a comic book." This statement tells Martin what is necessary, but does not imply that he is lazy.

In particular, one should refrain from using derogatory adjectives when pointing out the shortcomings of others. According to Ginott (1965), when parents call their child clumsy or stupid, the result is a chain of reactions that makes both the child and the parents miserable. A child who is repeatedly described in derogatory terms often begins to believe these things, and may behave in a manner that is consistent with these beliefs. In order to use criticism in a constructive manner, teachers should focus on the task to be done, avoid attacking the student's personality, and avoid derogatory comments. Teachers should also give criticism quietly, limit it to the situation at hand, and be brief with their remarks. Destructive criticism is unethical and unnecessary.

Timeout. Timeout, as you will recall from Chapter 5, is a behavior control technique that involves removing students from a reinforcing situation and placing them in a situation that does not provide rewards. Unfortunately, it is sometimes used with abandon, and then becomes an aversive technique. In extreme situations, children or adults have been isolated for hours or placed in dark or locked rooms. When timeout is harshly applied, students are deprived not only of social contact but also of basic human needs for long periods of time. In addition, the student's legal rights may be violated. Intense frustration and other emotional reactions may be associated with the process. As with any negative behavior control technique, care must be taken even when timeout is used with sensitivity. You should only use timeout if you have a good understanding of the method and its application. If you decide to use timeout, make arrangements for your program to be carefully monitored to insure that students are not being treated inhumanely.

Response cost. Response costs usually involve the loss of a privilege or points toward a grade as punishment for misconduct. The technique is a reasonable method for controlling behavior when it is properly used. For example, take care that minor infractions of rules do not result in extreme penalties. Failure to turn in homework on Tuesday should not result in loss of enough points to fail a student for the week. The fine or cost should be appropriate to the transgression. Earning an excessive fine on Monday would, no doubt, remove incentives for completing assignments for the remainder of the week. On the other hand, a very minor fine may result in no behavior change. Thus, a teacher must attempt to set a serious, yet fair, penalty when using this technique. It is especially important that the cost of misbehaving be specified in advance. The technique should not be suddenly applied at the whim of a teacher. For students to learn to control their own behavior, they must learn to appreciate in advance the consequences of certain actions. Erratic application of behavior control techniques deprives students of this opportunity.

The response-cost technique can be applied on a group basis as well as on an individual basis. Some teachers choose to use the procedure with their entire class. Using the technique on a group contingent basis raises ethical questions. Is it fair to penalize several children for the misbehavior of one child? Should group pressure be applied in changing an individual student's behavior? The group contingent response cost technique is generally a powerful one for changing behavior. However, it should only be used as a supplementary means of behavior control, when the behavior of several students needs to be changed at the same time. Further, group-contingent programs should be of short duration. Ultimately, each student should be required to deal personally with the consequences of his or her behavior.

Legal Issues Related to Negative Behavior Change Techniques

Timeout. In discussing timeout, Martin (1975) points out the importance of providing for due process (notice of intent to discipline, allowance of a period of time to prepare a defense, and a hearing) when isolation is imposed for disciplinary reasons. Fortunately, very few teachers consider long periods of isolation to be a good motivator of student behavior, but many recommend short periods in the timeout room. Martin suggests that if you can assure that "any administration of timeout as a motivating technique will not stretch to an hour or otherwise represent a substantial deprivation of liberty, then it might be used. If you cannot make that guarantee, then it should not even be attempted" (p. 86). Wherry (1983) outlines the following additional guidelines for the use of timeout: utilize the procedure only when the behavior of the student is substantially disruptive; provide lesson materials during the timeout period; and arrange for close and direct supervision. An educator who proposes to use timeout should be aware of the legal ramifications pertaining to its use. If the technique cannot be applied appropriately, it should not be used at all.

Corporal Punishment. The use of physical punishment raises not only ethical questions; legal ramifications may also arise from its use or misuse. The Supreme Court ruling in *Baker v. Owen* (1975) upheld a lower court opinion that schools have a right to use corporal punishment, under state law, even though the parents may object. In accordance with this ruling, procedural safeguards include: (a) give prior warning that certain behavior will result in corporal punishment; (b) arrange for another school official to witness the punishment; (c) tell the witness, beforehand and in the student's presence, the reason for the punishment; and (d) provide parents who request an explanation a written statement detailing the reasons for the punishment and the name of the witness.

A more recent Supreme Court ruling, *Ingraham v. Wright* (1977), held that the cruel and unusual punishment clause of the Eighth Amendment does not apply to corporal punishment when it is used as a disciplinary measure in the public schools. The Court further held that the due process clause of the Fourteenth Amendment does not require that notice and hearing be given prior to the imposition of corporal punishment as that practice is limited and authorized by common law (Englander, 1978). The Ingraham decision still holds and court decisions related to corporal punishment generally follow the precedent established in this case (Henderson, 1986). Nolte (1986) notes that the following principles apply in corporal punishment cases as handed down by the courts:

1. Teachers and principals must use professional judgment in administering corporal punishment within the guidelines established by the local school board. Parents may not legally prevent corporal punishment but are entitled to complete information after it has been administered.
2. If the punishment is unusually severe or excessive, parents can bring suit against the perpetrators for a jury to decide if excessive punishment was administered.
3. Corporal punishment is not unconstitutional.
4. School officials must be able to demonstrate in court that all other remedies short of corporal punishment were tried unsuccessfully prior to administration of corporal punishment.

Even in states where corporal punishment is not explicitly prohibited by state law, local ordinances may prohibit its use. Remember too, that although physical punishment may be permitted, it cannot be used indiscriminately. You should be aware that it is becoming increasingly common for parents to turn to the courts for redress in cases where they feel their child has been wronged or has been administered cruel and unusual punishment.

Corporal Punishment: A Basic Ruling

The use of corporal punishment as a disciplinary measure in the public schools remains a controversial issue. It was again brought to the attention of the courts when Ingraham, Adams, and other students at Drew Junior-High School, Dade County, Florida, charged they had been the victims of beatings that resulted in injuries ranging from a bleeding hematoma to a badly disfigured hand. A class-action claim was also included seeking relief against the use of corporal punishment in the Dade County School System. Following appeals through the lower courts, the case was heard by the United States Supreme Court in 1977. The Court held in Ingraham v. Wright *that the Eighth Amendment cruel-and-unusual-punishment clause was not applicable in this case.*

In writing the majority opinion, Justice Powell noted that schools are essentially open institutions where support of family and friends is available. Therefore, he reasoned, the student has little need of the protection offered by the Eighth Amendment. Justice Powell further noted that students' interests are adequately protected by state law. The first type of safeguard is prescribed by Florida statute and requires that the teacher confer with the principal before using corporal punishment on any student. The second safeguard results from the teacher's liability for civil damages in tort when corporal punishment that is unreasonable under the circumstances is used, and the third results from the teacher's liability for the crime of assault and battery if a child is physically harmed.

The issue of corporal punishment remains controversial. The court ruling was a close one (5–4) with the minority opinion taking issue with the arguments offered in the majority opinion. The debate on the use of corporal punishment did not end with the Ingraham v. Wright *decision.*

Legal Issues: Students' Rights

In the past, teachers and principals considered it their job to maintain discipline and to teach in the way they saw fit. Little attention was given to the rights of students or to the techniques used to maintain classroom control. This situation has changed in recent years. School personnel must now be aware of the legal implications of techniques used in the classroom. In fact, the constitutional rights of students represent one of

Freedom of Speech and the Press

The First Amendment's guarantee concerning freedom of speech and of the press applies to the student press. However, some differences exist in applying these rights to school newspapers based on a recent Supreme Court ruling. It was the opinion of the Court in *Hazelwood v. Kuhlmeier* (1988) that first amendment rights of students "are not automatically co-extensive with the rights of adults in other settings and must be applied in light of the special characteristics of the school environment." A significant body of case law exists that allows students to be disciplined for conduct or for actions associated with publishing and distributing materials. It has also been made clear that students have a legal responsibility to avoid activities that provide substantial or material disruption of the educational environment or which infringe on the rights of other students (Bartlett, 1984). Any student conduct that actually poses a damage to the safety or health of other students can be prevented by school authorities (Avery and Simpson, 1987).

Censorship and the Student Press

A recent ruling by the Supreme Court in Hazelwood School District et al. v. Kuhlmeier et al. *(No. 86-836, argued Oct. 13, 1987, decided Jan. 13, 1988) has implications for school-sponsored newspapers. In this case, former high-school students who had been staff members of the school newspaper filed suit in Federal District Court alleging that their First Amendment rights had been violated when two pages from an issue of the school newspaper were deleted by the school's principal prior to publication. The newspaper was produced as part of the school's journalism curriculum. The censored articles dealt with student pregnancies and parental divorce. The principal objected to the articles on the grounds that some of the people discussed in them might be identifiable and that the sexual nature of the material was, in his judgment, inappropriate for certain younger students. In addition, the principal contended that parents in the divorce article should have been given an opportunity to respond to the article or to give consent for publication. Because there was no time for further editing, the principal withheld publication of the two pages containing these articles even though the pages also contained other material.*

The District Court ruled that a First Amendment violation had not occurred in this case; the Court of Appeals reversed. The case was argued before the Supreme Court, which held that the respondents' First Amendment rights had not been violated. The opinion, delivered by Justice White, indicated that (a) the rights of students in public schools are not automatically co-extensive with rights of adults in other settings and that First Amendment rights must be applied in light of the special school characteristics; (b) the school newspaper in this case could not be considered a public-expression forum. School facilities are deemed to be public forums only if the school policy or practice is to open the facility for indiscriminate use by the general public or some segment of the public such as student organizations. In this case, the newspaper was produced in a journalism class and was not open to indiscriminate use by other student writers and reporters; and (c) educators do not violate First Amendment rights by exercising control over style and content of student speech in school-sponsored activities if the actions are legitimately related to concerns of a pedagogical nature.

Other Student Rights: An Overview

As a result of the *New Jersey v. T.L.O.* (1985: 743) case, teachers and other school officials may conduct searches and seizures on their own authority without a warrant if there is probable cause, based on the standard of reasonableness, to do so. (Lincoln, 1986). Lincoln offers the following recommendations for school officials who propose to conduct searches in their schools: (a) obtain and evaluate facts carefully prior to the search; (b) develop specific objectives for the search and seizure, and devise relevant procedures; (c) strictly follow the pertinent rules and regulations developed by the school district; (d) provide privacy for the search; and (e) keep complete and accurate records of the event.

Ornstein (1981) summarized several major constitutional rights of students that have been supported by court decisions and have relevance for educators. Educators should also be aware of the current status of students' rights in these areas.

Religious expression. This area remains controversial. Courts have declared the recitation of prayer, Bible reading, or the use of public school facilities for religious instruction unconstitutional. Attempts to change this stance have been made repeatedly in Congress and the possibility exists that court ruling may be changed at some time in the future.

Symbolic and personal expression. The Supreme Court has upheld students' rights to wear buttons, armbands, decals, and other symbols of personal expression as long as the manner of expression does not materially intrude upon the rights of others or the orderly process of the school.

Assembly and petitioning. Students may organize clubs or associations within schools for political as well as social or athletic reasons. Membership cannot be denied due to race, religion, sex, or other reasons unless the rules of the school disqualify some applicants. Demonstrations, picketing, and collection of signatures is allowed with the limitations that these activities cannot be disruptive and cannot occur when dangerous conditions exist.

Academic penalties and grades. Unless the infraction is related to academic dishonesty, punishment should not affect students' grades, credits, or graduation. A diploma cannot be denied because a student has broken a rule of discipline. Reducing grades for absences is a questionable practice. In general, courts do not challenge teachers' grades that are based on academic performance. Mixing academic performance with behavior, however, could create problems. At present there appears to be no clear consensus on the legality of reducing grades for disciplinary reasons, but the trend of court decisions appears not to favor this policy (Bartlett, 1987).

Pregnant and married students. Basically, students cannot be denied an education or restricted from normal graduation exercises because of pregnancy or marriage.

Exclusion from extracurricular activities. There must be a legal basis for barring students from full participation in extracurricular activities. States vary with regard to the extent of disciplinary exclusion that is allowed, but generally, it cannot be arbitrary, capricious, or unreasonable.

Police in schools. In general, police are allowed to enter schools only if a crime has been committed, if they have a warrant for an arrest or search, or if they are invited by school officials. Some states permit police more latitude, but still ensure that the constitutional rights of the students are preserved. That is, students must be advised of their rights, and they have the right to ask their parents for advice or to seek counsel.

Rights of Parents

In recent years, parents have become more aware of their legal rights in the areas of student discipline, instruction, and school records. For example, parents now have the right to see all school records on their child and to challenge any record they feel is unfair or untrue. Teachers should be aware that parents do have these rights with regard to their child. This should generate more objectivity when compiling student records. Teachers should be very careful about making any assumptions, and record only facts. Objective records not only benefit the child but also minimize disagreements when parents examine school records.

Cautions for Teachers

Teachers' liability for actions in the classroom is an increasing area of concern. Not all teachers are aware that they can be held liable for negligent conduct. According to Ripps (1975) the same principles and rules of law that apply to negligence when a teacher acts in a private capacity also apply to a teacher in the classroom. That is, teachers must provide the same standard of professionalism as would a reasonable and prudent person who is acting under the same circumstances. If a breach of duty causes damage or injury, the teacher can be held liable.

Most court actions involving the supervisory role of teachers have been taken against teachers who were absent from the classroom when a student was injured. Therefore, adequate supervision should be provided when it is necessary to leave the classroom. To help provide protection in the legal sense, evidence of a well-developed plan for adequate supervision should be maintained at all times. Risks are particularly high in gym and laboratory classes. Teachers must supervise properly *and* prevent injury. It is extremely important that instructions be given regarding basic procedures for equipment and other potential dangers. Failure to provide necessary safety equipment can result in liability; so can poorly maintained equipment (Ripps, 1975).

Intentional actions for which teachers may be held liable primarily involve physical interference with the student. Assault and battery arising out of the teacher's disciplinary actions have comprised the majority of court suits. Teachers should consider their actions carefully. Attempting to force your "will upon a student without the authority of at least written rules and regulations is acting foolishly" (Ripps, 1975, p. 22). Teachers cannot always rely on their institution for support.

The influence of the courts on the conduct of teachers and administrators cannot be predicted at this time. Issues continue to arise which may eventually be settled by the courts. Teachers should keep abreast of new developments and the ramifications of these developments on their own actions in the classroom.

Accountability

Undoubtedly, teachers and other school personnel will eventually have to become accountable for making changes in student behavior. Unfortunately, the goals of many schools and teachers are often so elusive as to make accountability impossible. For example, how can a teacher measure whether a second grader has learned to be a good citizen? Cox (1977) argued that teachers are unable to control outcomes of teaching, and it is therefore unfair to hold them accountable. For example, he feels that "school-ability," a student trait composed of several elements such as intelligence, attitudes toward school, self and others, language ability, and social class has more influence on the outcomes of instruction than the teacher's instructional methods. In his view, holding teachers accountable for molding behavior would foster a lower quality of education because teachers would be likely to set lower-level goals than could be achieved.

Raybin (1979) avoided the controversy over teachers' accountability for outcomes of instruction by suggesting that educators be held accountable for developing and implementing basic instructional programs in the various subject areas. Under his plan, a program of minimum essentials, by semester and grade level (or course title), would be developed by a responsible person in order to provide students with a certain amount of knowledge in the field. These minimum essentials would be agreed upon by teachers in the subject areas and would require only 40 to 50% of class time for mastery by the average student. The plan would allow significant time for other teaching activities by each individual teacher. Because there is no guarantee that students would eventually learn the material, accountability under Raybin's plan is seen to rest upon implementation rather than outcomes of the program.

It may not be possible, however, for educators to ignore the issue of instructional outcomes and focus on implementation of specified programs as suggested by Raybin (1979). Two court cases (*Peter W. v. San Francisco Unified School District,* 1976, and *Donohue v. Copiague Union Free School District,* 1979) have dealt with the issue of whether schools are liable when students fail to learn what is taught. While the judgments in these cases did not find the schools liable for malpractice, the risk remains that educators may eventually be held accountable if they do not attend to instructional outcomes for individual students. Epley (1985) offers three possibilities for dealing with this issue: (a) establishing quality-control arrangements to review and monitor the progress of each child at each organizational level; (b) setting up an appeals process for dissatisfied students; and (c) developing individualized educational plans for all students modeled after those for exceptional children. It seems clear that educators will need to study the accountability issue in depth and develop workable strategies for dealing with its many facets.

Teacher evaluation is another issue that has resulted from the growing demand for teacher accountability. In general, the courts have held that there are few, if any, objective criteria for assessing teacher performance or for determining just grounds for dismissal (Webb, 1983). As a result, each case must be individually assessed. Although educational malpractice has not held up in court to date, in view of current legal logic, this may change if educators do not attend to quality-control issues for individual children (Epley, 1985).

"After an exhaustive study of your new curriculum which evaluated all available data, using multivariable longitudinal analysis with particular attention to IQ, SES, and academic-cognitive and affective-social factors as they relate to state goal-orientation, I find that you were doing it better before."

Webb (1983) states that effective evaluation practices and due-process rights of teachers are not in conflict. Due-process issues are consistent with the goal of evaluation, which is to improve instruction. Due process is also concerned with fairness. Webb suggests that the following elements of fairness be incorporated into evaluation policies: (a) the teacher should know the performance standards and the criteria and procedures to be used in evaluation; (b) evaluations should be performed within reasonable time frames; (c) adequate notice of evaluation results should be provided; (d) if an employment decision or remedial correction is needed, the teacher should be provided with direction for correction; (e) the teacher should be allowed a reasonable amount of time to carry out the prescribed improvement; (f) the teacher should be given a chance to improve; and (g) the evaluation should be a type that provides substantial evidence for employment decisions. Peterson (1983) stresses that due process; nondiscrimination due to race, religion, national origin, sex, or handicap, and validity and reliabilty of the evaluation measures are important issues to consider. The amount of judgment required by the rater in measuring performance criteria must also be considered.

Regardless of the controversy among educators concerning accountability, it is conceivable that the public will increasingly hold educators accountable for making specific changes in students' behavior. Setting precise goals and documenting students' progress will not only assist in teaching but can also provide information for accountability. While higher-order goals may be more difficult to specify, teachers can subdivide these goals into component parts. Judging achievement of any level goal rests on observable behavior. The task of the teacher is to define what the student will be doing when the goal has been mastered.

Summary

This chapter focused on ethical and legal implications related to the use of behavior management techniques in the classroom. Guidelines for the ethical use of these techniques were also presented. Specific ethical questions concerned with behavior change include: should behavior management techniques be used to induce conformity and who should make the decisions regarding the behavior to be changed? Questions pertaining to positive behavior change methodology include: is it ethical to use tangible rewards; does a reward procedure teach desirable values;

and is tangible reinforcement equal to bribery? Ethical questions arising from the use of negative behavior change techniques arise mostly from the use of corporal punishment, criticism, timeout, and response cost. Problems related to the use of these techniques were discussed.

The discussion of legal implications related to the use of behavior management techniques stressed the importance of educators' awareness of new developments in this area. Due process, equal protection under the law, and accountability should be meaningful to every educator. Specific problems that could be encountered with the use of reward systems and timeout were delineated, as were actions for which a teacher might be held liable. The 1975 and 1977 Supreme Court decisions pertaining to corporal punishment were discussed, and educators were cautioned to set school policies that are harmonious with existing laws and court rulings. The 1988 Supreme Court ruling regarding censorship of the student press was also addressed.

Finally, issues pertaining to teacher evaluation and accountability were discussed. The latter issue, in particular, has increasingly become a concern of the general public. The need for educators to develop plans for dealing with both accountability and teacher evaluation was stressed.

Legal Issues Review

A. To accord students' due process:
   1. Give prior notice that a behavior is prohibited.
   2. Give notification when a penalty is to be applied.
   3. Give students information concerning the charges against them.
   4. Allow students the opportunity to respond to the charges.
   5. Provide for a hearing regarding the charges and insure a fair decision.

B. To provide for equal protection:
   1. Treat all students substantially the same.
   2. Make sure that discernible groups of student are not excluded from activities without justification.

C. To consider legal ramifications of behavior change techniques:
   1. Individualize behavioral interventions.
   2. Obtain informed consent of the parents or guardians before using a specific technique such as timeout.
   3. Try other behavioral strategies before placing a student in a more restrictive environment.
   4. Document student progress.

5. Redesign ineffective interventions.
6. Limit use of procedures incorporating use of timeout and punishment.

D. To consider legal issues of positive reward systems:
   1. Allow students to earn extra rewards.
   2. Allow students the basic rights to remain free of manipulation.
   3. Allow students to retain personal property.

E. To consider legal issues of timeout:
   1. Provide for due process.
   2. Use timeout only for short periods of time.
   3. Use the procedure only when the student's behavior is substantially disruptive.
   4. Provide lesson materials during the timeout period.
   5. Arrange for close and direct supervision.

F. To consider legal issues of corporal punishment:
   1. Give prior warning that certain behavior will result in punishment.
   2. Arrange for another school official to witness the punishment.
   3. Tell the witness beforehand and in the student's presence the reason for the punishment.
   4. Provide parents a written statement upon request detailing the reasons for the punishment and the name of the witness.

References

Avery, K. B., & Simpson, R. J. (1987). The Constitution and student publications: A comprehensive approach. *Journal of Law and Education, 16,* 1–61.

Baker v. Owen, 423 U.S. 907 (1975).

Bartlett, L. (1987), Don't mix: A critical review. *Journal of Law and Education, 16,* 155–165.

Bartlett, L. (1984). *Student press and distribution issues: Rights and responsibilities*. Reston, VA: National Association of Secondary School Principals.

Bentley, K. J. (1987), Major legal and ethical issues in behavioral treatment: Focus on institutionalized mental patients. *Behavioral Sciences and the Law, 5,* 359–372.

Cox, B. C. (1977) Responsibility, culpability and the cult of accountability in education. *Phi Delta Kappan, 59,* 761–766.

Donohue v. Copiague Union Free School District, 47 N.Y. 2d440, 418 N.Y.S. 2d.375, 391 N.E. 2d1352 (1979).

Englander, M. E. (1978), The Courts' corporal punishment to parents, local authorities and the profession. *Phi Delta Kappan, 59,* 529–532.

Epley, B. G. (1985), Educational malpractice: The threat and challenge. *The Educational Form, 50,* 57–65.

Gault, 387 U.S. 1 (1967).

Ginott, H. G. (1965). *Between parent and child,* New York: Macmillan.

Goss v. Lopez, 419 U.S. 565 42 (1975).

Hazelwood School District v. Kuhlmeier. 86–836 U.S. S. Ct. (1988).

Henderson, D. J. (1986). Constitutional implications involving use of corporal punishment in the public schools: A comprehensive review. *Journal of Law and Education, 15,* 255–269.

Hickman, M. J. (1986). The Supreme Court and the decline of students' constitutional rights: A selective analysis, *65,* 161–187.

Ingraham v. Wright, 430 U.S. 65 (1977).

Lehr, D., & Haubrich, P. (1986). Legal precedents for students with severe handicaps. *Exceptional Children, 52,* 358–365.

Lincoln, E. A. (1986). Searches and seizures. The U. S. Supreme Court's decision on the Fourth Amendment. *Urban Education, 21,* 255–263.

Martin R. (1975). *Legal issues in behavior modification.* Champaign, IL: Research Press.

New Jersey v. T. L. O., 105 S. Ct. 733 (1985).

Nolte, M. C. (1986). Before you take a paddling in court, read this corporal punishment advice. *American School Board Journal, 173,* 27, 35.

O'Leary, K. D., Poulos, R. W., & Devine, V. T. (1972). Tangible reinforcers, bonuses or bribes? *Journal of Consulting and Clinical Psychology, 38,* 1–8.

Ornstein, A. C. (1981), Student rights for secondary students: An overview. *Contemporary Education, 52,* 214–218.

Peter W. v. San Francisco Unified School District, 60 Cal. App. 3d814, 131 Cal. Rptr. 854 (1976).

Peterson, D. (1983). Legal and ethical issues of teacher evaluation: A research based approach. *Educational Research Quarterly, 7,* 7–15.

Piele, P. K. (1978). Neither corporal punishment nor due process due: The United States Supreme Court's decision in Ingraham v. Wright. *Journal of Law and Education, 7,* 1–19.

Raybin, R. (1979). Minimum essentials and accountability. *Phi Delta Kappan, 60,* 374–375.

Ripps, S. R. (1975). The tort liability and the classroom teacher. *Akron Law Review, 9,* 19–33.

Ritchie, R. M. (1973). Due process and the principal. *Phi Delta Kappan, 54,* 697–698.

Webb, L. D. (1983). *Teacher evaluation.* Reston, VA: National Association of Secondary School Principals.

Wherry, J. N. (1983). Some legal considerations and implications for the use of behavior modification in the schools. *Psychology in the Schools, 20,* 46–51.

CHAPTER 9

Keeping Track: Helping Students Manage Their Own Learning Behavior

"I'm almost overwhelmed by the complexity of our world these days. Do you think our students will be able to cope with the rapid changes in the future?"

"Only if we teach them the skills they need to deal with a complex and changing society. In other words, they need techniques for lifelong learning and responsible citizenship."

The preceding chapters have emphasized things teachers can do to manage students. There are also a number of important reasons for teaching students how to manage themselves effectively. First, students who develop the skills to acquire new knowledge and to monitor their own proficiency levels should be able to function more effectively in a variety of settings (Bradsford, Sherwood, Vye, & Rieser, 1986). Thus, teachers may actually have a broader, more significant, influence by teaching students to govern themselves. Second, students may perform better both socially and academically when given opportunities to manage themselves. Research relating to perceived opportunities for self-managed learning and perceived academic locus of control has suggested that students are likely to accept responsibility for academic successes and failures if they perceive the classroom as a place where they can play a part in managing their own instruction (Arlin & Whitley, 1978). Third, students are often the only ones in a position to know what changes are needed. Teachers can never hope to know the inner thoughts of students, nor can they expect to see everything that happens in and out of the classroom. Also, students may know better than the teacher what is reinforcing and punishing. Desired changes are possible only when meaningful consequences are provided for desired behavior. Finally, many of the ethical and legal problems involved in the use of various rewards and punishments can be avoided when students take part in decision-making processes.

Many benefits are obviously associated with the development of self-management skills. Of course, self-management never completely frees a student of dependence on others. Support, encouragement, and feedback from teachers and others will always be needed. Students must also be taught how to use specific self-management strategies. This chapter focuses on providing support for students as they learn to manage important areas of their lives including social behavior, comprehension of text materials, and use of effective study techniques.

"You call bugging the teachers' lounge leadership qualities?"

Social Self-management

The techniques discussed in Chapters 4 and 5 describe ways that teachers can manage student behavior, but many of the same techniques can be used by students to change their own behavior and achieve self-control. In this section, we will discuss the most prevalent techniques for self-management of social behavior: self-recording; control of setting events; managing consequences; self-verbalization; and behavioral contracting. Although we will discuss each technique separately, they can be used in combination. Students will probably benefit from learning all of the strategies and then selecting what seems most natural and effective.

Self-recording

Students are often unaware of how they actually behave. Some of their behavior may occur so automatically that it completely escapes their attention. Other behavior by itself may seem too unimportant to notice. However, by recording their own actions, students can become more aware of how they appear to others. Such information alone may be all that is required to produce a change in behavior.

Broden, Hall, and Mitts (1971) found that self-recording was effective in increasing an eighth-grader's attention to classroom lessons. In a second experiment, Broden and her colleagues found that self-recording also reduced talking without permission by another eighth-grader, but in this case, self-recording eventually lost much of its effectiveness. The researchers suggested that external support might be needed to sustain the behavior changes initiated through self-recording. They commented that "perhaps the most promising feature of self-recording will be to use it as a procedure for initiating desirable levels of appropriate behavior to a point where the teacher can more easily reinforce the desired behavior with attention, praise, grades, or other reinforcers available in the classroom" (p.198). Of course, when desirable behavior changes become habitual, self-recording and reinforcement can be gradually reduced.

Other researchers have reached similar conclusions. Sagotsky, Patterson, and Lepper (1978), for instance, found self-recording was effective among a group of fifth- and sixth-graders for increasing the amount of study time and rate of progress through an individualized mathematics program. In the self-recording phase of that study, the students periodically marked a plus or a minus on grids to indicate whether they were actually studying math. The procedure reminded students to continue study.

Still other researchers have found that self-recording can be effective with special education students. Long and Williams (1976), for example, employed self-recording with a group of retarded adolescents. Each student had to maintain a point sheet on which points were recorded for appropriate responses. The students logged points for being ready to start lessons, having appropriate materials, completing assignments, working quietly for specified time periods, and similar activities. Recording of points increased levels of appropriate responding for the group by approximately 10% during spelling and by approximately 15% during reading.

Although self-recording may prove beneficial for many students, several research studies (Bolstad & Johnson, 1972; Long & Williams, 1976; Mahoney, Moura, & Wade, 1973) reveal that it can be more effective when combined with other techniques. Teachers can use self-recording with external reinforcements, with other self-management techniques, or with both. The potential usefulness of self-monitoring to maintain behavior that has been established through other intervention strategies, such as peer-monitoring, has also been demonstrated (Fowler, 1986). Teachers should recognize, however, that self-recording is not foolproof. It may work best for those students who seek help and who are already highly motivated to change.

Methods of Recording. The methods selected for record-keeping will depend largely upon the behavior being monitored. Behavior that has a distinct beginning and end lends itself to a frequency count. This involves nothing more than counting the number of times the behavior occurs. Number of positive and negative comments, questions asked or answered, times late for class, and similar behavior can be subjected to a frequency-count assessment. Paper and pencil or a mechanical counter can be used by students to make frequency counts.

Some behavior that occurs over extended time periods does not readily lend itself to a frequency count. Time spent studying, working on special projects, sleeping, being off the task, and similar behavior can best be evaluated by "time assessment." The simplest way to assess time spent on a task is with a stopwatch. Rather than making a continuous frequency count or an assessment of all the time spent at a specific behavior, a student could be assisted in sampling a behavior at designated intervals. Sampling can provide valuable information if a behavior occurs frequently enough so that periodic measures are representative of the student's total behavior pattern.

will usually recognize immediately that their behavior does not occur in a vacuum. The most important point for them to learn, though, is not why they behave as they do, but that something can be done to change their behavior.

Generally, teachers want to control setting events to either reduce the stimuli that trigger unwanted behavior, or increase the stimuli that foster desired behavior. Students who refuse to bring nonacademic materials to class (unless requested to do so) reduce the range of stimuli that could generate unwanted behavior. Similarly, students who elect not to sit beside friends who encourage inappropriate talking, who limit the distractions occurring during their study time, or who avoid associating with peers who insist on misbehaving are reducing the probability of misbehaving. Because students cannot always avoid troublesome situations, they may have to concentrate on increasing the stimuli that foster desired behavior.

Strengthening desired behavior, of course, will also invariably reduce unwanted behavior. Shy students who associate with people who encourage socializing increase the probability of overcoming their shyness. Likewise, students who bring appropriate texts and materials to class and who develop a schedule for their daily activities increase the stimuli that can cue appropriate behavior. With the teacher's help, they can probably think of numerous other stimuli that can be altered for better control of their own behavior.

Managing Consequences

Although self-recording and control of setting events alone may produce changes in behavior, these techniques are often most helpful when combined with managing behavioral consequences. It is the events that occur following behavior that largely determine whether the behavior will occur again. To maintain desired changes that result from self-recording, control of setting events, or other techniques, teachers should help students manage the consequences of their own behavior.

Several studies have found self-managed reinforcers superior to teacher-managed reinforcers. Lovitt and Curtiss (1969), for example, found that the academic response rate of a 12-year-old student was higher when the student specified the requirements for reinforcement than when only the teacher specified the requirements. Similarly, Bolstad and Johnson (1972) revealed that self-regulation of reinforcers (self-recording and self-dispensing of reinforcers) was more effective in reducing inappropriate behavior among the most disruptive students in 10 first- and second-grade classrooms than was teacher regulation of reinforcers. Other studies (Ballard & Glynn, 1975; Long & Williams, 1976) attest to the potential usefulness of self-rewards. More studies (e.g., Arwood, Williams, & Long, 1974) suggest that students' input into deciding upon punishment can improve their behavior. In fact, Grusec and Kuczynski (1977) found that children can be taught to punish themselves. Pease and Tyler (1979) found that self-management of timeout duration is as effective as teacher-management in reducing the rate of disruptive behavior.

Reducing Disruptive Behavior through Self-management

Brigham, Hopper, Hill, De Armas, and Newsom (1985) describe a self-management program that was used successfully over a three-year period to reduce the disruptive behavior of adolescents in a middle-school setting. Initial participants consisted of 103, primarily male, sixth-, seventh- and eighth-grade students. Of the 103, 79 students completed the self-management program. Most of the 79 participants were described as immature or impulsive and their infractions tended to consist of relatively minor classroom disruptions. A minority (14) of the participants were reported to have serious behavior problems and were described basically as "calculated rule breakers." Six students exhibited problems with truancy.

Students in this study qualified for the self-management class when they reached a criterion of 12 detentions for infractions of school and classroom rules. The program involved hour-long classes three days a week for six weeks. In addition, completion of a self-management project was required of each student. Once the required skills were mastered, participants planned and implemented self-management projects that included a behavioral-problem analysis, specific written intervention steps, and a behavioral contract between the student and the self-management instructor. In each project, the students were encouraged to select a key behavior to increase or decrease. The major dependent variable was detention following a rule violation.

Taken as a whole, the results of the three-year program suggested that students could reduce their frequency of detentions through self-management procedures. In addition, follow-up data of the program indicated that a significantly lower frequency of detentions occurred with the self-management group in the year following their participa-

tion in the class. Although the program was not successful in altering the behavior of all participants in the desired direction, it suggested that for some students behavioral self-management represents a viable approach in dealing with disruptive adolescents.

Teachers who are interested in having students manage behavioral consequences need to consider a number of factors for such a program to be a success:

1. Because accurate management of reinforcers and punishers requires record-keeping, students may need assistance in developing record-keeping systems. The previous discussion on self-recording should be helpful in this respect.
2. Research suggests that individuals reinforce themselves in much the same way as they have been reinforced by others (Kanfer & Duerfeldt, 1967). Thus, teachers may find that they can increase student success with self-reinforcement by first successfully reinforcing desired student behavior. Teachers who find that students are either too lenient or too stringent with rewards and punishers may want to consider how they themselves are responding to the students.
3. Students may need assistance in identifying appropriate reinforcement and punishment. Atkins and Williams (1972) found that students often have difficulty identifying stimuli that actually serve as reinforcers. Perhaps this is a result of limited exposure to a variety of potential reinforcers. In any case, students must realize that something is reinforcing only if it will maintain or strengthen behavior for them. Teachers may find that by having the entire class make a list of potential reinforcers, the likelihood that each student identifies appropriate reinforcers will be increased. Likewise, students may require assistance identifying potential punishers. Many students probably think that punishment consists of a paddling, a trip to the principal's office, or suspension. They may never have considered the possibility of withholding a privilege, overcorrection, or other forms of punishment. Students should receive instructions in the effective use of reward and punishment. For example, applying reinforcers contingent on desired behavior, applying them immediately, and using a variety of reinforcers are

just as applicable when self-applied as when externally controlled. Students can achieve success with self-management of consequences only to the extent that they know how to control those consequences properly.

Self-verbalization

From time to time, most people instruct themselves vocally or subvocally on what they should and should not do in given situations. Guevremont, Osnes, and Stokes (1986) found that preschool children who were taught to verbalize the behavior in which they were to engage showed improved behavior not only in the experimental setting but also in temporally and spatially remote settings. Results of this research suggested that a training procedure to develop consistency between children's verbalizations and subsequent behavior could be potentially useful to teachers in modifying students' behavior. Athletes, for example, often tell themselves, "watch the ball," "wait for the signal before starting," or "keep your head down." Similarly some motorists, when caught in a line of traffic, remind themselves to "be patient," "remain calm," or "try to be courteous to other drivers." There are also occasions in the classroom when self-verbalization could help students achieve better self-control. Students can verbalize to themselves to control anger, reduce anxiety associated with giving a speech, and be more positive in the comments they make to others.

An interesting study by Meichenbaum and Goodman (1971) demonstrated that a group of second graders who were exhibiting hyperactive and impulsive behavior could be trained to talk to themselves as a means of developing self-control. They were trained on a variety of tasks, such as copying line patterns and coloring figures within boundaries. During the training sessions, students individually observed the experimenter perform the task while giving himself instructions aloud. The following is an example of the experimenter's self-verbalizations:

> Okay, what is it I have to do? You want me to copy the picture with the different lines. I have to go slowly and be careful. Okay, draw the lines down, down, good; then to the right, that's it; now down some more and to the left. Good, I'm doing fine so far. Remember go slowly. Now back up again. No, I was supposed to go down. That's okay. Just erase the line carefully . . . Good. Even if

I make an error I can go on slowly and carefully. Okay, I have to go down now. Finished. I did it (p. 117).

After observing the experiment, each student performed the task while giving self-instructions aloud. Next, the student performed the task while whispering instructions. Finally, the student performed the task silently (without lip movements). The idea was to help students internalize self-instructions. The students who received training in self-verbalization subsequently performed significantly better on psychometric tests which measured cognitive impulsivity, performance IQ, and motor ability than did control students who were exposed to the training tasks, but were not trained to self-verbalize.

Behavioral Contracting

Behavioral contracting is a technique that appears to be widely used with students of vastly different backgrounds. The real value of contracting, however, does not lie in its potential to alter problem behavior, but in its provisions of means by which students can progress from external control of their lives by others toward greater degrees of self-management. Contracting enables teachers and students to reach *mutual agreements* in which students can assume more control as they demonstrate greater personal responsibility. Clark (1978), in a study involving 150 adolescent students, found that most students considered the contracts used in the study fair and worthwhile and they preferred them to other teaching methods. Students gave the following reasons (ranked by frequency) for enjoying the contracts: (a) allows individuals to work at their own pace without being nagged; (b) provides knowledge as to what is expected of students; (c) allows students to improve their course grade; (d) allows independent work; (e) provides an opportunity to earn free time by completing work; (f) allows students to receive individual teacher attention; and (g) allows students the opportunity to choose from a variety of activities.

Contingency Contracting with Disadvantaged Adolescents

Kelley and Stokes (1982) evaluated the effects of a student-teacher contracting procedure on the academic productivity of disadvantaged *adolescents. Research subjects were 13 students enrolled in a vocational-educational training program for disadvantaged students between the ages of 16 and 21 years. All participants were junior-high or high-school dropouts. Participants received vocational training and academic preparation for the high-school-equivalency diploma as well as $2.35 for each hour they attended school. Minimal control over the participants' behavior in the academic-skills setting was reported by the program administrator prior to the initiation of the study. Students were said to complete little or no work.*

The major dependent measure in the Kelley and Stokes (1982) study was the number of workbook items completed by the students and the percentage of the completed items that was correct. The study involved four phases: Baseline I; Contracting I; Baseline II; and Contracting II. During the baseline phases, students completed exercises in a self-paced workbook and were paid each Friday based on their attendance. Just prior to the contracting phases, participants were informed that their pay would now be earned according to the number of correct workbook items completed daily. They were given the opportunity to earn as much as they had previously received for attendance. A self-management strategy was employed in that each student negotiated a contract with the teacher for the following week. The teacher continued to grade all student work according to scoring rules in the baseline conditions.

Kelley and Stokes (1982) found that student-teacher contracting with pay contingent on contract fulfillment was effective in increasing the productivity of the disadvantaged youths involved in the program. Anecdotally, it was noted that the contingency also increased task-oriented behavior of the students. The teacher reported that contracting required minimal time to administer while students reported a preference for contracting because the amount of work that they were to accomplish was clearly delineated. Some students also reported a greater sense of accomplishment during the contracting phases.

One of the most practical plans for using contracting to help students achieve greater self-control has been developed by Homme, Csanyi, Gonzales, and Rechs (1970). Their plan embodies five stages. The first is labeled manager-controlled contracting: An adult manager (e.g., teacher) determines the task to be performed and the amount of reinforcement to be given for completion of the task. Upon acceptance of the contract by the child and completion of the assigned task, the manager delivers the reinforcement. In the second stage, the child may be given joint control of the task or of the reinforcement. If the child assumes partial control of the task, the manager maintains complete control of the reinforcement. If the child jointly controls the reinforcement, the manager determines the task. You will notice that at this stage greater control is still maintained by the adult manager.

The third stage allows equal control by the manager and the child. The child can: (a) jointly control the task and the amount of reinforcement; (b) completely control the task, while the manager controls the amount of reinforcement; or (c) control the amount of reinforcement, while the manager controls the task. The fourth stage shifts even more control to the child. The child can take complete control of the task while jointly sharing control over the reinforcer, or can take complete control over the reinforcer while sharing control of the task. In the fifth and final stage, labeled "child-controlled contracting," the child has control over both the task and the reinforcer. Homme and his colleagues (1970) suggest that students achieve success with each stage and with each possible type of control before advancing to the next stage. Their plan appears to have considerable merit because it allows a gradual transition to self-control as students demonstrate ability to assume new responsibilities.

Both teachers and students can exercise varying amounts of control in contracting, but you may still be wondering about some of the mechanics of implementing a contract: whether it should be positive or negative, whether it should be used with individuals or groups, and how to obtain student participation. First, although contracting can consist of agreements to do or not to do certain things, we believe that it should emphasize positive behavior. This does not mean that rewards should never be withdrawn for misconduct, but contracts that clearly identify appropriate behavior and the payoffs for that behavior should be far more acceptable to teachers and students. The contracting process can be greatly simplified by remembering that the same principles of reinforcement discussed in Chapter 4 and mentioned in this chapter (managing behavioral consequences) should be followed, no matter who controls the contract.

Second, contracts can be effective whether they are used with individuals, small groups, or large classes. You will probably find that using the same format for an entire class is less demanding than developing unique instruments for each student. Of course, the tasks that students perform and the reinforcement they select can vary without having different contracts. Students can simply be given a choice of rewards once they have completed their assigned task.

Finally, to involve students, a straightforward approach is best. We ask them to define appropriate and inappropriate classroom behavior and what the consequences (reward and punishment) should be for each kind of behavior. Students can also be involved in the wording of written contracts, in maintaining records, in providing feedback on the success of the contracting, and in making recommendations for new ways of using contracts. Besalel-Azrin, Azrin, and Armstrong (1977) found that a program that maximized student responsibility resulted in fewer classroom problems as reported by students, teachers, and independent observers. Students at all grade levels will have ideas to share if their teacher is willing to solicit and reinforce student input. Possibly the most important consideration in implementing a contract is the teacher's willingness to involve students. After all, contracting connotes cooperation.

Although you and your students could devise many different types of contracts, an illustration of a behavioral contract negotiated between an eighth-grade teacher and her students is shown in Figure 9.2. Perhaps, you and your students would be interested in trying a similar contract in your class.

Keeping Track of Study Behavior

Keeping track of social behavior is important. It is also crucial that students learn to manage their study habits effectively if they are to achieve mastery of content subjects in elementary and high school as well as college. As students move from the primary grades to more advanced levels the requirement for independent learning skills becomes greater. Very often, however, they lack the mature study strategies that are needed to master work at a higher level.

Simpson (1984) cites three explanations for deficiencies in students' study strategies: (a) they have not been instructed in adequate study techniques; (b) they cannot self-regulate (i.e., plan activities, monitor and revise strategies, and evaluate outcomes) those strategies that they may know; and (c) they may not understand how to apply a learned strategy to a new task. In addition, students may forget to use strategies they have learned.

In view of these problems, Simpson (1984) offers a number of recommendations to help educators develop plans for teaching study strategies. The first recommendation is comprehensive and must be

FIGURE 9.2
CONTRACT FOR CLASSWORK

I agree to abide by the following conditions and consequences during Math 101. I understand this agreement will be renegotiated after a trial period of three weeks or before that time if a majority of students or the teacher feels another agreement would be more desirable.

Conditions:

1. To be seated and ready to begin work before the tardy bell rings.
2. To bring pencil, paper, and appropriate books to class.
3. To avoid engaging in loud talking, noise making, and other behavior that could interfere with others' learning.
4. To complete class assignments each day and correct all errors on previous day's assignments.

Consequences:

Free time will be available for approximately 10 minutes at the end of each class period for those who have met all the preceding conditions for that day. During free time, eligible persons may read comics, draw, listen to the radio (if earplugs are used), play math games provided, work on other assignments, or engage in other relaxing activities that do not disturb others. Those who do not meet the conditions or those who disturb others during free time must begin their homework assignment or proceed with other assigned tasks.

signed:

____
(student)

____
(teacher)

implemented at a systems level. That is, district-wide committees should be developed to research and discuss whether study strategies are being taught, what they are if they are being taught, whether the strategies being taught are relevant, and whether the strategies are taught in multiple and realistic contexts. Recommendations can then be made concerning curriculum changes based on the answers to these questions.

Addressing the issue of study strategies for the classroom teacher is also important. At this level, Simpson suggests that teachers provide direct study instruction that includes: (a) formulating rules and steps for particular strategies and sharing these rules and steps with the students; (b) modeling the thinking process that a student might use to apply the rules to a particular study task; and (c) providing the students with opportunities for guided practice in the study technique, perhaps through checklists.

Simpson (1984) also stresses that elementary and middle-school teachers in science and social studies should reinforce the study skills taught in language arts and that junior-high and high-school teachers should take the time to teach the study strategies that are appropriate for their own subjects. Teaching study skills is not the domain of the language-arts teacher only. Students must learn to apply the skills that are most effective for each subject area. The time required of teachers to help students become proficient should be well repaid.

Steps in Summarization

Students should be taught to summarize what they read. Brown, Campione, and Day (1981) developed the following rules for teaching students how to summarize:

1. *Leave out trivial or unimportant information.*
2. *Leave out redundant information.*
3. *Group items or actions under a general label.*
4. *Choose (or invent, if necessary) topic sentences in paragraphs.*

To teach students to use these guidelines Brown, Campione, and Day (1981) suggest the following strategies:

1. *Give direct explanations and explicit instruction.*
2. *Give students opportunities to practice.*
3. *Have students monitor or evaluate their summaries to determine whether they followed the rules.*

Two specific study skills, summarization and self-questioning, appear to be particularly effective in the language arts and content areas. "Summarization" requires that students be able to discriminate between more and less important information in a text. The summarizing technique involves having students read text passages, develop summary statements based on the information presented in the text, and record or write the summarized information. King, Biggs, and Lipsky (1984) found that summarizing produced higher scores on an essay test than did a self-questioning procedure and was also as effective as self-questioning in answering objective questions in their study. King, Biggs, and Lipsky's approach to summarizing was quite comprehensive, however, and required that students recognize not only the main ideas but also relevant details in a passage. Thus, the high scores on the objective test in the summarization group may have been partly a function of this attention to detail.

Self-questioning has also emerged as an effective study technique for some subjects. André and Anderson (1978–79) found that students learn more when they generate their own questions about textual material than they do with a rereading procedure. Training students in the self-questioning technique also seemed to improve their skills in generating good comprehension questions and subsequently produced better answers to questions on a criterion test. André and Anderson suggested that students with lower ability may benefit more from self-questioning than students with higher ability.

King, Biggs, and Lipsky (1984) also found self-questioning to be a useful study technique for students. These researchers formulated the following conclusions from their study:

1. Students should be told early on about the format of tests to be given so that their study strategy can be matched to testing. For example, summarization may be more effective in studying for essay tests and self-questioning may be more beneficial for objective tests.
2. The strategies should be reviewed and taught in the classroom. Teachers should tell students what is and is not important during classroom discussions.
3. Teachers should follow-through on such discussions by testing students' knowledge of important facts, not trivial detail. Students who are told to remember important facts and are then tested over trivial detail may not undergo the mental exercise required for comprehensive mastery of the material. Instead, they will probably resort to rote memorization.

Tips for Self-questioning

Teaching students to ask questions prior to and during reading can be a helpful strategy in promoting comprehension. Listed are examples of questions developed by Mangano, Palmer, and Goetz (1982) that students might find useful when studying for tests:

1. *Who are the main characters (in a story)?*
2. *What happens in the story?*
3. *Where does the story take place?*
4. *What do you predict will happen next in the story?*
5. *What is the main idea (in factual texts)?*
6. *What details explain the main idea?*
7. *What questions might be asked on a test, and what are the answers to these questions?*
8. *What might the next reading section be about, based on what has already been read?*

Learning to summarize effectively and to generate relevant questions can undoubtably improve students' study skills. Another technique that has utility in the self-management of study involves monitoring the actual amount of time spent studying. Students using this technique may be surprised to learn that more time is devoted to nonstudy behavior, such as getting organized, eating a snack, or listening to a record, than to actual study. Monitoring on-task study time could thus provide clues to failures in mastery of assigned material. Keeping records of increases in study time and resultant effects on academic achievement can also provide incentives for developing regular study habits. Further, having a defined purpose or goal to be accomplished in each study session and speculating on the positive outcome of the study sessions could increase student motivation for productive study. Teachers can help students keep track of their study habits by assigning record-keeping tasks and asking students to set study goals that are reviewed weekly by the teacher.

Monitoring Thought Processes

How well do students keep track of their own thought processes? One aspect of thinking that has received a great deal of attention in recent years is "metacognition," that is, a fundamental aspect of thinking that involves an awareness of personal cognitive processes and how to translate this awareness into workable strategies when one does not understand what is being taught (Lloyd & Loper, 1986). Applied to school students, metacognition means that they must first understand what they need to know to perform a task, and then develop a new strategy or employ an existing one to use the information that they already have toward solving the problem (Lloyd & Loper, 1986).

While metacognition appears to involve an overall understanding of thought processes, a somewhat less encompassing term, "metacomprehension," is often used to describe the awareness and self-control of strategies that are useful for increasing comprehension (Fitzgerald, 1983). Metacomprehension is especially important for reading and understanding content. The focus of research on reading in recent years, for example, has reflected educators' long-term concern for teaching students how to derive meaning from what they read (Davey & Porter, 1982). Monitoring reading comprehension requires that students develop an awareness of the quality of their understanding (Pitts, 1983) and is considered essential for competent reading skills (Wagoner, 1983).

Pitts (1983), in summarizing research on reading comprehension, reports that older, better readers monitor comprehension more effectively than younger, poorer readers. Lloyd and Loper (1986) further indicate that much information is available to indicate that underachievers are metacognitively deficient. Poor comprehenders seem to form opinions quickly, do not shift ideas in response to new information, and are unable to describe strategies that would be helpful in altering their deficiencies (Davey & Porter, 1982). Davey and Porter, in training middle-school students who were poor comprehenders, found that these students tended to focus on decoding and were easily distracted, especially during silent reading. The poor comprehenders also felt that time would take care of the problem and that they would understand better as they got older. In contrast, effective readers and learners develop strategies for regulating their own comprehension (Davey & Porter, 1982).

It cannot be assumed that all students have the skills necessary for keeping track of their progress in reading comprehension. Tierney (1982), following a review of several studies, concluded that students can be taught to monitor their own comprehension provided the teaching plan is carefully developed. Tierney offers five guidelines for developing successful instruction: (a) determine whether the strategy is worth teaching. Certain strategies may be a hindrance rather than a help for certain reader purposes; (b) inform students as to the why, when, where, and how of a given strategy; (c) provide students with opportunities to explore and develop their own guidelines; (d) guide students toward independence or self-regulation in the use of the techniques; and (e) provide opportunities for generalization.

Several procedures for helping students monitor reading comprehension have been proposed. Mangano, Palmer, and Goetz (1982) suggest that monitoring reading comprehension might be improved by teaching students to use prereading questions to help them develop hypotheses and a purpose for reading. Davey and Porter (1982) suggest that teachers should demonstrate and model strategies for monitoring comprehension and describe how they handle problems with comprehension by using specific examples. Pitts (1983) proposes that an instructional program on monitoring comprehension should familiarize students with common obstacles to comprehension, teach them to ask questions related to their own awareness, and give them remedial strategies to deal with comprehension failures. ''Fix up'' strategies suggested by Pitts include to first ignore lack of comprehension and read on unless large sections of the text are incomprehensible. In the case of comprehension failure, Pitts suggests slowing down the reading rate. If the first two strategies do not work, Pitts recommends withholding judgment and/or forming a hypothesis to be tested with further reading. A fourth strategy, rereading, is proposed if the reader notices contradictions or perceives too many possible interpretations. The last strategy, consulting an expert source, is judged as the least desirable technique because it's disruptive and wastes time.

Involve the Students

''Reciprocal Teaching'' (Palinscar, 1986) is the name given by A. S. Palinscar and A. Brown for a metacognitive teaching strategy that is aimed at helping students derive meaning from texts. Reciprocal teaching involves a dialogue between students and the teacher. Palinscar describes four activities that characterize the dialogue:

1. *Summarization in which the main ideas of the text are identified and paraphrased.*
2. *Self-questioning concerning the type of information from the text that could be found on both comprehension and recall tests.*
3. *Clarification when a breakdown in comprehension has occurred followed by the necessary action to restore meaning (e.g., rereading, asking for help).*
4. *Generating hypotheses based on the structure and content of the text.*

In using the reciprocal-teaching method, the teacher initially assumes primary responsibility for the dialogue. Each day of the instruction, however, the teacher attempts to gradually transfer responsibility to the students by providing feedback and coaching. Success is achieved when students are able to assume control of the strategy.

Palinscar (1986) makes two very important points concerning the selection of materials for use with the reciprocal-teaching procedure. One, the students should be able to read the material without encountering many decoding problems. Two, the material selected should be similar to the type of material students must study and read in school.

Educational literature abounds with information on metacognition, metacomprehension, and comprehension monitoring. Strategies for teaching comprehension monitoring are described in detail in professional journals such as *Journal of Reading, The Reading Teacher, Journal of Reading Behavior,* and *Reading Research Quarterly.* In these journals you may also find information about other techniques such as rereading, paraphrasing, and reading related to personal experience. Teachers are encouraged to consult these journals for new ideas.

Being unable to monitor comprehension can interfere with effective reading and also with learning in the content areas. We have discussed several strategies for teaching students how to keep track of their own comprehension. Lloyd and Loper (1986) also suggest three general steps for remediating metacognitive problems: (a) assess through interview, observation, or questionnaire whether the student has a problem. Interview and observation are best for classroom use; (b) develop a treatment plan based on the information obtained through assessment; (c) maximize the effectiveness of intervention by "trouble-shooting."

Trouble-shooting should give attention to the following questions: (a) are the instructions explicit?; (b) are the tasks demanding enough?; (c) are the task too demanding, that is, is the interview tailored to the level of the student?; (d) is the strategy appropriate to the task or does it interfere?; and (e) are students kept informed of their progress?

Summary

Successful self-management by students is an important educational goal. We believe that students do not learn self-responsibility when their affairs are continuously managed by others. They also do not learn effective self-management skills when total control is thrust upon them. Students learn self-management the same way that they learn other tasks:

teachers must help students become aware of alternative ways for achieving self-control and provide opportunities for students to use those techniques. Self-recording, setting events, managing reward and punishment, self-verbalization, and contracting were discussed as the principal techniques of self-control. A number of important concerns that teachers raise about self-control were also discussed. In addition, techniques for helping students keep track of their study behavior and monitor their comprehension of test material were offered. Concern, encouragement, and positive responses from others will be needed as students learn to become more independent. Coupled with external support, the learning of self-management skills is unlimited in value.

SELF-MANAGEMENT CHECKLIST

Did you remember to:	Yes	No	Results and Recommendations
A. Teach specific self-management techniques:			
1. self-recording.			
2. setting events.			
3. managing consequences.			
4. self-verbalization.			
5. behavioral contracting.			
B. Evaluate use of self-control methods on:			
1. student behavior.			
2. student achievements.			
3. ease of implementation in the classroom.			
C. Instruct student in how to study effectively by:			
1. formulating rules and steps for particular study techniques and sharing these guidelines with the students.			
2. modeling the thinking process for applying particular study techniques.			
3. providing students with opportunities for guided practice in the study techniques.			

Long, J. D., & Williams, R. L. (1976). The utility of self-management procedures in modifying the classroom behaviors of mentally retarded adolescents. *Adolescence, 41,* 29–38.

Lovitt, T. C., & Curtiss, K. A. (1969). Academic response rate as a function of teacher and self-imposed contingencies. *Journal of Applied Behavior Analysis, 2,* 49–53.

Mahoney, M. J., Moura, N. G. M., & Wade, T. C. (1973). The relative efficacy of self-reward, self-punishment, and self-monitoring techniques for weight loss. *Journal of Consulting and Clinical Psychology, 40,* 404–407.

Mangano, N., Palmer, D., & Goetz, E. (1982). Improving reading comprehension through metacognitive training. *Reading Psychology, 3,* 365–374.

Meichenbaum, D. H., & Goodman, J. (1971). Training impulsive children to talk to themselves: A means of developing self-control. *Journal of Abnormal Psychology, 77,* 115–126.

Palincsar, A. (1986). Metacognitive strategy instruction. *Exceptional Children, 53,* 118–124.

Pease, G. A., & Tyler, V. O. (1979). Self-regulation of time-out duration in the modification of disruptive classroom behavior. *Psychology in the Schools, 16,* 101–105.

Pitts, M. (1983). Comprehension monitoring: Definition and practice. *Journal of Reading, 26,* 516–523.

Sagotsky, G., Patterson, C. J., & Lepper, M. R. (1978). Training children's self-control: A field experiment in self-monitoring and goal-setting in the classroom. *Journal of Experimental Child Psychology, 25,* 242–253.

Simpson, M. (1984). The status of study strategy instruction: Implications for classroom teachers. *Journal of Reading, 28,* 136–143.

Tierney, R. (1982). Essential considerations for developing basic reading comprehension skills. *School Psychology Review, 11,* 299–305.

Wagoner, S. (1983). Comprehension monitoring: What it is and what we know about it. *Reading Research Quarterly, 18,* 328–344.

CHAPTER 10

Putting It All Together

Establishing effective classroom discipline is no simple matter. Many variables operate in every classroom, making it impossible to provide a single solution to every challenge. In addition, effective classroom management seldom results from making just one change in the classroom. Successful management requires that teachers look objectively at each situation and alter whatever is needed to establish and maintain optimal conditions for learning. Such objectivity can probably be best achieved by having a broad understanding of different disciplinary strategies as well as an understanding of how different strategies can be pieced together to yield a consistent approach.

This chapter will look at ways in which the ideas presented in the previous chapters can be organized into a unified approach. We will apply the ideas to the solution of two common classroom problems, then we will give you the opportunity to see how well you can do with specific problems.

General Review

Chapter 1 suggested that, although problems are an integral part of teaching, the major thrust in teaching should be aimed at influencing students in a positive direction rather than aimed at merely stopping problems. It was proposed that teachers examine the expectations they bring to teaching as an initial step in moving toward effective classroom management. Chapter 2 then turned to a discussion of teacher actions that demonstrate concern for students' well-being and that, in effect, help to establish the rapport needed for a proper learning environment.

While the first two chapters largely emphasized how teacher behavior influences classroom dynamics, Chapters 3 and 4 looked at ways in which other variables can be used to enhance learning. Chapter 3 stressed how

"Cheer up, John—Not everyone gets the hang of class control the first time."

various prompts (such as the establishment of goals, rules, and procedures) can be used to increase the likelihood of desirable behavior. Chapter 4 told how desired behavior, once exhibited, could be strengthened through reinforcement. In essence, the strategies described in Chapters 3 and 4 should be combined to help students develop appropriate academic and social behavior. For example, the strategies in these two chapters should be useful in working with students who fail to complete assignments, interact minimally in class activities, attend school irregularly, or are not reaching their full potential in other ways.

Although enhancing desirable student behavior can do much to avert problems, it is not the total answer to classroom management. Among other things, teachers need strategies for dealing with inappropriate behavior that occasionally occurs in every class. Chapter 5 presented a variety of intervention strategies that have been used successfully in managing inappropriate behavior. The strategies in Chapter 5 seem most applicable to problems such as disruptiveness, aggressiveness, defiance, and similar actions that interfere with the learning process.

Classroom problems are frequently influenced by factors outside of the classroom. The need for greater cooperative efforts between the school and the home was emphasized and practical ways of achieving better home-school relationships were discussed in Chapter 6. In the same vein, Chapter 7 noted that teachers sometimes face difficulties that are outside their area of training. We suggested that a working relationship be established with the resource staff in the school in order to meet the needs of exceptional students. Chapters 6 and 7 emphasized that no one can meet every challenge alone. Seeking assistance from parents and colleagues is a sign of maturity, not of weakness.

Chapter 8 described the ethical and legal issues involved in managing a modern-day classroom. The special attention given to ethical and legal issues underscores our belief that only classroom procedures that recognize the rights and dignity of every person can ultimately accomplish the high goal of enriching the lives of students and teachers.

Finally, Chapter 9 suggested that student involvement also plays a major role in effective classroom management. Students' desire for independence becomes especially acute as they grow older. Students, like most of us, like to feel they have a measure of control over what happens to them. Moreover, students are expected to manage their own lives after they finish school. The emphasis in Chapter 9 was on a planned program to give students more responsibility for directing their lives as they demonstrate greater self-management abilities.

Approaching Actual Problems

Effective classroom managers don't simply react to a problem as it unfolds. They typically have a systematic plan for preventing as well as resolving problems. Not all effective managers use an identical approach, but effective classroom management usually entails some of the elements from each of the preceding chapters.

Chapters 1 through 9 constitute a model for managing most classroom difficulties. Our model includes:

1. Set reasonable expectations.
2. Act in ways that demonstrate concern for yourself and for others.
3. Have a program to enhance desired behavior (Chapters 3 and 4) as well as a program for reducing disruptive behavior (Chapter 5).

4. Work cooperatively with parents.
5. Work cooperatively with resource personnel.
6. Use only strategies that meet the highest ethical and legal considerations.
7. Move students toward greater self-responsibility.

Naturally, some problems will involve greater emphasis on one or more of these points than others. For example, if you have determined that your students rarely exhibit behavior that could enhance their achievement and self-worth, you would rely heavily upon prompting and reinforcement. Perhaps you should involve students more in establishing goals, rules, and procedures, and assess and use their interests to make learning more enjoyable. A change in materials might also be needed or a variation in the ways lessons are presented. You would avoid punishment, of course, because punishment is intended to suppress inappropriate behavior, not strengthen desired responses. You might also want to examine the expectations you have for the students (Chapter 1).

As you formulate these plans, you should examine your own attitudes. Perhaps you should involve parents or others. You also want to make sure that you do not violate your own conceptions of right and wrong or fail to adhere to any school policies. Finally, try to move the students toward self-management of their own behavior. Similarly, if the problem is one that disrupts learning activities, you would be just as thorough in applying each of these positive reinforcement procedures, but you might also legitimately include procedures that would suppress inappropriate actions.

With this format as our model, let us now look at a way of solving two different problems: one in which students are not reaching their potential and another in which there is behavior that disrupts the learning process. We will make a number of suggestions from each chapter. You can use those suggestions that seem most appropriate for you and your students.

Motivating Students To Complete Assignments

Ms. Wong, a fifth-grade teacher, has a problem ''motivating'' students to complete assignments. TV, sports, and other competing student interests seem to rank higher on her students' priorities than school work. Students frequently do not complete class assignments. ''I know they are busy, but too many fail to complete their classwork'' is how Ms. Wong described her class. What do you think can be done?

Set reasonable expectations. In assessing her own expectations, Ms. Wong might wish to ask herself whether the beliefs she holds are in any way affecting students' behavior. For instance, does she believe that all students should naturally want to do school work in preference to other activities? If so, perhaps that notion restricts the approaches that Ms. Wong takes to make the work more interesting. Her attitude towards nonschool activities might give her negative feelings toward those students who don't show as much interest in school work as she'd like.

Act in ways that demonstrate concern. Assuming Ms. Wong recognizes that her students come to her with varied interests and motivation to learn and that she is not placing unreasonable demands on them, we might ask what is she doing to demonstrate concern for herself and her students? Is her own life in balance? That is, is Ms. Wong so busy with school work that she never takes time to relax or pursue healthful activities outside of school? Could a hobby or nonschool activity improve her classroom management skills?

In considering Ms. Wong's problem, we also asked ourselves what she might be communicating to her students. Is she telling them through verbal and nonverbal messages that outside activities are always less important than their homework? Does she consider special events when she gives assignments? Does the way she personally relates to extracurricular events influence how students perceive her? Does she let the students know through her actions that she is as concerned about them as she is about what they are not doing? Of course, we have no absolute answers. However, by asking herself these and similar questions, Ms. Wong might come up with some ideas that would be helpful.

Enhance desired behavior. Teachers want to motivate students to complete assignments; therefore, the emphasis should be on prompting and reinforcing desired actions as opposed to punishment. While there are many plausible explanations for the behavior of Ms. Wong's students, we wondered if the students could actually do the work that was being assigned. Could some of her students have been assigned inappropriate books? Does she need to simplify her instructions? Does she need to link some of her assignments to outside student activities? You could probably think of other questions for Ms. Wong that might suggest how to prompt more of what she wants from her students.

Although this was never stated in her explanation of the problem, we hypothesize that Ms. Wong's students find little reason for completing assignments. Yes, they may fail for not doing them, but a good grade for performing or the threat of a poor one for nonperforming may be insufficient to motivate many students. There must be a meaningful reward for everyone. Ms. Wong must be just as enthusiastic about the completion of assignments as she is concerned about noncompletion, perhaps even more so. She has to recognize and reward improvement. We are not implying that Ms. Wong is the sole problem. The solution is to find appropriate ways of cueing student performance and insuring that students get reinforced for their efforts. Then, the students will want to perform. They will have a good reason for doing so.

Work with parents. Students' failure to complete homework assignments immediately suggests a need to increase the involvement of parents. Ms. Wong might be able to use some of her parents as tutors, aides, or resource people. Or, she might wish to develop a cooperative program with some parents to provide reinforcement to students at home for work completed at school. Judicious use of the telephone, "Happy-Grams" (positive notes to parents about a student's performance), and home visits might improve the school situation. Certainly, all of these suggestions take time, but the alternative is the continuation of the problem. Often the initial expenditure of a little time eventually results in time saved.

Work with school resource personnel. By using the techniques described in earlier chapters, Ms. Wong can probably increase homework completion without outside consultation; however, school specialists such as the school psychologist or counselor can provide assistance. Possibly Ms. Wong could use assistance in establishing a reinforcement program for her class. Perhaps she could benefit by discussing "what's new" in classroom management with colleagues or others. Maybe someone else can respark the old interests that led her into teaching.

Use only strategies that meet the highest ethical and legal considerations. Ethical and legal issues must be considered when examining the strategies she chooses to achieve the desired ends. If external rewards are being used, she should have a plan for phasing-out those rewards. Long-term use of any extrinsic, artificial-reward system can diminish the value of performing a task for the joy of learning. Students should be asked what personal pleasure they receive from a task well done. They should be helped to assess their pride in achievement and not be asked to do something indefinitely because it makes the teacher proud. Ms. Wong should also consider personal accountability. If students do not complete the required assignments, will they be able to attain an adequate mastery of the subject matter?

Move students toward greater self-responsibility. Having students perform work assignments without being prodded is an important goal in education. Unfortunately, some students will always require more nudging than others, but most are capable of achieving fairly high degrees of self-responsibility. Of course no one ever becomes totally independent of others. It may well be that students do not know how to study and monitor their own progress. Students should be taught effective study and self-monitoring procedures. Many teachers also find contracting to be an effective way of moving away from a teacher-dominated to a student-teacher controlled environment. In schoolwork contracts, students can share in specifying assignments and the payoffs for performance and nonperformance. Another relevant strategy is self-recording. By logging the time they spend studying, watching TV, and engaging in other activities, students often realize the need for changing their behavior. Still another approach is to increase student input in class discussions. Maybe Ms. Wong is too much the center of the class. Many students have the attitude that, when someone else makes all the decisions, that person can also do all the work. Perhaps you have other thoughts on moving students toward greater self-responsibility.

Reducing Student Defiance

Mr. Johansen, a first-year teacher, had been experiencing increasing difficulties with a number of his math students. Early in the year, he related well with them and they worked hard in class. They appeared eager to please him. As time passed, he noticed that some students were becoming less compliant with his requests. They would murmur among themselves, laugh at his requests, and take their time doing what he asked. Sometimes they would ignore him, acting as though they could not hear what he said.

Mr. Johansen initially avoided taking any action, hoping the situation would improve. He was afraid that he would earn a reputation as not being able to handle his classes; however, he realized something had to be done when one of his students made an obscene gesture after being asked to stop talking. Assume you are the teacher: What can be done?

Set reasonable expectations. Although Mr. Johansen should not accept open defiance, he must remain willing to examine his own beliefs and behavior if he hopes to resolve the problem. His fear that he might get a bad reputation suggests that he subscribes to the view that "good teachers don't have problems." We feel that he should abandon this conception to avoid thinking of himself negatively and, in turn, acting negatively toward others.

Act in ways that demonstrate concern. Regardless of whether the problem is one of getting students to perform a desired task or to refrain from misconduct, teachers should assess whether they are acting in ways that imply that they don't care about their students. Perhaps a change in behavior can steer student-teacher relationships in a positive direction.

The following questions might help clarify how teachers' actions influence student defiance:

1. Has an individual student done something in the past to make you more suspicious of all the students' actions?
2. Do you act in ways that communicate that you must be the boss?
3. Have you, perhaps unconsciously, built situations that will increase the probability of confrontation?
4. Are you willing to admit mistakes?
5. Do you use an indirect approach when dealing with defiant students? That is, do you respond to the feelings behind their overt behavior?
6. Do you know and communicate something good about each student? (Direct defiance of your authority is less likely when students feel you are interested in them).
7. Do you put misbehavior in perspective? (Students who defy your authority may have little against you personally. Realizing this, you may respond more calmly.)

Reduce inappropriate behavior. Managing behavior that disrupts learning activities may involve nonpunitive as well as punitive techniques. Nonpunitive strategies typically include procedures designed to increase behavior incompatible with undesirable behavior. In Mr. Johansen's class, it would be a good idea to increase cooperative student behavior. Strategies should be designed to reinforce cooperation, model desired actions, and change the setting events in such a way that defiance is prevented. Negative intervention techniques might also be used to deal temporarily with extreme acts of defiance.

Mr. Johansen could select a combination of the following management strategies to remedy his situation:

1. Make an effort to notice when students cooperate, and verbally praise this behavior.

2. Make sure students understand that praise and rewards are tied to cooperative behavior. Immediately reward students who cooperate.
3. When a student seldom cooperates, shape cooperative behavior by rewarding behavior that approximates the goal of full cooperation.
4. Model expected behavior. That is, tell students why you are following certain policies yourself and demonstrate how you comply. You should also avoid behaving in aggressive ways.
5. Avoid giving commands that you have no authority to enforce or that you would be unable to enforce if confronted. It is better to ask students to do something than to tell them what they are going to do.
6. Try to deal with inappropriate behavior privately (a change in setting events). Little can be accomplished when opposing individuals are forced into a confrontation while other individuals are watching. If the student complies with your request to accompany you out of the room, try to find a place where the student can sit quietly and "cool off" before you attempt to discuss the problem. This time will also allow you to make arrangements for your other students.
7. Direct your attention at the student's feelings and reasons for defiance rather than at the overt behavior itself. For example, you might say, "You believe I should not have asked you to stop talking at this particular moment," or "You feel I have been unfair with you today." If the student responds positively to your empathy, the door may be open for talking about the problem. In effect, you have started a behavior change process by withholding attention for inappropriate actions while reinforcing appropriate expression.
8. When a teacher's authority is challenged, the problem is usually not confined to one student and the teacher. Other students in the class may also become emotionally involved even though they do not overtly act out their feelings. To avoid having students take sides and possibly reinforce defiance by directing attention to the problem, we suggest that you focus student attention on assignments. Say, for example, "We have work to do; this is between . . . and me." You might also consider having a group meeting at a later time to discuss how peer attention influences class behavior.

9. If a student is obstinate about staying in the class and is threatening you, it may be necessary to ask for assistance from the school administrator. However, the basic problem cannot be solved by the principal or vice-principal. The problem remains between you and the student. The principal may be required to remove the student for a temporary period (timeout), but you should personally work out the problem with the student after allowing a cooling-off period.
10. Avoid using harsh punishment or suggesting to the principal that the student be suspended. A positive approach incorporating some curtailment of privileges, but allowing the student to overcome the incident without extreme action, is preferable. Suspension may be viewed by the disinterested student as a holiday rather than punishment.

Work with parents. Any time a problem with a student appears to be escalating, you should talk with the parents. You could indicate that you and their child are having difficulties, and get their suggestions for dealing with their child. Talking with parents can avert subsequent disgreements over why they have not been advised earlier should the necessity for punishment arise. Mr. Johansen's problems might never have occurred had he established a good relationship with his students' parents. Students are more likely to cooperate when you are on positive speaking terms with their parents. In Mr. Johansen's case, the chances are his student's parents will come to him if he waits much longer.

Work with school personnel. Try consulting with the school counselor or psychologist when you are confronted with a defiant student. If the problem has been going on for some time without resolution, you may need objective analysis from another professional. You might ask the counselor to observe your interactions with the students and give you suggestions for possible changes. The counselor can help Mr. Johansen consider how he makes requests and the fairness of demands he is placing on students.

Use only strategies that meet the highest ethical and legal considerations. Chapter 8 discussed how many classroom management problems could be averted if teachers would carefully consider the ethical and legal implications of their actions. Indeed, much student defiance could be a direct result of their feeling that they are not being treated as they should be.

In considering the problem of defiance, ask yourself:

1. Is the defiance a result of my attempts to create unnecessary conformity? Do I give the students ample opportunity to question classroom goals?
2. Have the techniques (either positive or negative) I am using generated defiance? Would an alternative approach be just as acceptable without creating a similar problem?
3. Have I recognized the rights of the students? Are they being treated as I would treat adults? Have any basic privileges that students are entitled to by right been withheld?
4. Are some students being treated "more equally" than others?

Move students toward greater self-responsibility. No teacher can eliminate defiance without the cooperation of the students. Frequently, defiant students wish they had never challenged others, but they lack the knowledge for achieving greater self-control. At other times, students may become defiant simply because they have been excluded from decision-making processes.

We suggest that the students be given the opportunity to:

1. Help set events and examine reinforcers that may be precipitating and controlling their behavior.
2. Consider the merits of self-verbalizations. (This tactic seems extremely appropriate for helping students practice more acceptable ways of expressing themselves.)
3. Develop behavioral contracts for appropriate classroom behavior.

On Your Own

No simple solution exists for managing classroom difficulties, and you may wonder which specific techniques should be applied when several options are available for remedying a problem. For instance, when immediate action is needed, which technique should be used: a soft reprimand, timeout, or response cost? The answer depends on your setting, your students, and your own preferences. Some school administrators may ask that certain techniques be avoided. The age of your students might preclude frequent use of certain techniques. Also, your experience with a student may reveal that one technique will work while another technique does not. You may simply prefer one strategy over another. Probably, however, you will use most of the techniques with different students at different times.

We think you should be familiar with as many alternatives for changing behavior as possible, and you should be prepared to deal with a variety of problems. For this reason, we are offering a number of simulated classroom problems to allow you to practice working through different incidents before facing them in class. Imagine yourself as the classroom teacher who must deal with each of these common problems.

Just as we did on the problem of defiance, we suggest that you peruse Chapters 1 through 9, selecting the techniques you believe most appropriate for each problem. Remember to: (a) set reasonable expectations for yourself; (b) act in ways that demonstrate concern; (c) select your classroom strategies on the basis of whether the problem represents a need to strengthen or weaken a behavior; (d) work cooperatively with parents; (e) use all available resources in your school; (f) maintain the highest ethical and legal practices; and (g) work toward helping students achieve self-responsibility for their behavior.

1. Marie is a young, attractive, high-school physical-education and health teacher. Frequently, she comes from a physical education class to a health class in gym shorts because she doesn't want to change clothes three to four times each day. Several of the mature boys in class have been making remarks about her good looks. She is afraid things are going a little too far. What can she do?
2. Christy is a very quiet, shy, and withdrawn fifth grader. You observe that she is a loner in class and that she does not approach other students. In addition, she is not approached by them. She seems to be an unhappy child. As her teacher, you are concerned about her inability to interact with her peers. What can you do to help her?
3. You notice that your eighth-grade students are apathetic during history class. They seldom comment and then only in response to your direct questions. What can you do?
4. Scott tends to assume a threatening posture and is often verbally aggressive to other seventh graders. In particular, he engages in name-calling and brags about beating up other boys if they bother him. How can this problem be resolved?

5. Andrea and Deborah are close friends. During class periods, they continually whisper and pass notes. Some of the other students complain that they cannot work because the whispering disturbs them. How can you deal with students who talk during class activities?

6. Several of your fourth-grade boys are loud and boisterous during lunch. Their table manners are usually poor, and some days worse than others. For example, they throw bread and swap food, sometimes overloading their plates. The students' behavior disrupts your own lunch. How can you create a calmer, more enjoyable lunch period for everyone?

7. George and Randy run to tell you that two of your fifth-grade boys are fighting on the playground. This is not the first time that the boys have become involved in fights during recess. You do not wish to have the fights occur again. What can you do to deal immediately with the behavior, and how can you prevent fights in the future?

8. Leroy appears to have good intentions about doing his school work; however, he seldom completes an assignment. You realize that something should be done to change his behavior. Analyze and provide suggestions for this common problem.

9. You enter your room on Friday to find desks overturned, walls decorated with writing, and papers strewn over the floor. You are distressed at the wreckage, but must continue the day as usual. You feel, however, that something should be done about the vandalism problem. What are some things that you, as a teacher, might do?

10. Two of your tenth-grade girls are consistently tardy to history class. They give one excuse and then another for being late. You want to give them the benefit of the doubt, but you are convinced that their excuses are invalid. What can you do to reduce their tardiness?

11. Your fourth-grade students tend to run in the school halls unless directly supervised. In addition to being unsafe, this behavior is disruptive for other classes. You certainly do not wish to have it continue. What can you do to eliminate this problem?

12. Several of your students are reported to create disturbances on the school bus. In particular, they push and shove and refuse to share seats with others. Is there anything you can do to reduce this behavior, even though you do not ride the bus?
13. Several students report that their school supplies and personal clothes have been "ripped off" at school. Problems with stealing appear to be increasing. What are some ways you might eliminate the thefts?
14. It is becoming increasingly apparent that drugs and alcohol are problems for some of the students in your class. The problem obviously cannot be solved by ignoring it. What are some constructive ways to approach it?
15. You have been given a teaching assignment as a twelfth-grade English teacher in an inner-city school. You find that students tend to group together, and that there is no interaction between the various racial groups in your classroom. How would you approach this problem?
16. You have been asked to supervise a fifth-period, high-school study-hall class. You know that several boisterous students have been assigned to this class. Therefore, you are concerned that you will be unable to maintain order and to deal with problems that may arise. However, you have no choice but to carry out this assignment. What are some ways that you might approach the study hall in order to minimize problems?
17. Juan, a young teacher, is having difficulties with several of his eighth-grade girls. They follow him around, want to talk with him in private, pass notes to him, and in general let him know that they like him a lot. Juan wants to be friendly, but he realizes that he must do something to establish the proper relationship with these girls. What can he do?
18. One of your ninth graders, Jay, is absent from school more frequently than he is present. You are concerned about his truant behavior. What can you do to help keep Jay in school?

Concluding Comments

Classroom management problems have always existed, and no one is suggesting that teachers can prevent every problem. Some problems are simply the result of normal interpersonal interactions. Most teachers experience much joy in helping others overcome difficulties and move toward greater self-control.

It is one thing to face an occasional problem and another to live inundated with problems. Too many teachers tell us the latter situation characterizes life in today's classrooms. No one deserves such a fate. We think teachers can improve circumstances by becoming more aware of the techniques now available for improving most classrooms. But awareness alone will not make a good teacher. You must have the courage to apply what you know. The goal of our book has been to increase your knowledge of classroom management techniques. To be useful, these techniques must also be applied in the daily management of your classroom.

Index